Dr Jackie Huggins AM FAHA, a member of the Bidjara and Birri Gubba Juru peoples, is currently leading the work for Treaty/ Treaties in Queensland. In popular demand as a speaker on Aboriginal issues, she is a well-known historian and author, with articles published widely in Australia and internationally. Her acclaimed biography of her Mother, *Auntie Rita*, was published in 1994. Keeping it in the family, in 2022 her biography of her Father, *Jack of Hearts: QX11594* will be published.

She was the former Co-Chair National Congress of Australia's First Peoples, former member of the National Council for Aboriginal Reconciliation, Co-Chair Reconciliation Australia, the State Library Board of Queensland and the Australian Institute of Aboriginal and Torres Strait Islander Studies. She was Co-Commissioner for Queensland for the Inquiry into the Separation of Aboriginal and Torres Strait Islander Children from Their Families, and for several years was a judge of the annual David Unaipon Award.

JACKIE HUGGINS

SISTER GIRL

REFLECTIONS ON TIDDAISM, IDENTITY AND RECONCILIATION

UQP

First published 1998 by University of Queensland Press
PO Box 6042, St Lucia, Queensland 4067 Australia
This edition published 2022
Reprinted 2022 (twice)

University of Queensland Press (UQP) acknowledges the Traditional Owners
and their custodianship of the lands on which UQP operates. We pay our respects
to their Ancestors and their descendants, who continue cultural and spiritual connections
to Country. We recognise their valuable contributions to Australian and global society.

uqp.com.au
reception@uqp.com.au

Cover design by Christabella Designs
Cover and author photograph by Connie Kotze
Typeset in Bembo Std 12/16 pt by Post Pre-press Group, Brisbane
Printed in Australia by McPherson's Printing Group

 University of Queensland Press is supported by the
Queensland Government through Arts Queensland.

  University of Queensland Press is assisted by the
Australian Government through the Australia
Council, its arts funding and advisory body.

A catalogue record for this book is available from the National Library of Australia.

ISBN 978 0 7022 6547 1 (pbk)
ISBN 978 0 7022 6664 5 (epdf)
ISBN 978 0 7022 6665 2 (epub)
ISBN 978 0 7022 6666 9 (kindle)

University of Queensland Press uses papers that are natural, renewable and recyclable
products made from wood grown in well-managed forests and other controlled sources.
The logging and manufacturing processes conform to the environmental regulations of
the country of origin.

MIX
Paper | Supporting
responsible forestry
FSC
www.fsc.org FSC® C001695

for my Mother Rita
the inspiration of my life

and my truest Sister Girl,
Ngaire

Contents

Preface

I have always considered *Sister Girl* among my strongest writings. This is the book I did for me. When some have been offended by it, others have applauded. At 65 years of age now I have learnt not to wallow in the self-pity of criticism or being popular or liked. Frankly I am over it. My ego is in check and does not suffer any longer. Take it or leave it these days.

Some twenty-four years after *Sister Girl* was first published, the best compliment anyone can give me is that I am older and wiser just like my beautiful Mum, who would have turned 100 years of age last year. A day does not go by without thinking of her, her inspiration and teachings. A truly universal spirit. This time I also dedicate this book to my Number One right-hand woman and truest Sister Girl in every sense, my Sister Ngaire Jarro.

In the 1990s I had a scholarship at the Australian Centre, Melbourne, where I wished to probe what kind of 'feminism' our Aboriginal women possessed. I began thinking about this in the 1980s when I was a university student. Of course, I would never presume to speak for Torres Strait Islander women. Now that's a book waiting to be written.

At the Australian Centre there were two Aboriginal women students studying and we were able to explore and exchange some worthwhile ideas around feminism and how it relates to Indigenous peoples. The students and I had an affinity with the word Tidda. This is an endeared universal term used by Aboriginal women for 'Sister' or 'woman'. It needs no explanation as it is a cherished declaration. The Victorian singing group Tiddas were raging then, having wide success across the country at this time

Personally, Tidda is a term that has been in our family and knowledge base for as long as I can remember. In fact my favourite niece from Cherbourg and Murgon is called Tidda, aka Desma Fisher/Tita. Tidda is an 'in' word for me, whereby I prefer only Indigenous women use it.

Coincidentally, my time at the Australian Centre was when I wrote my first solid criticism of the then-called 'white women's movement'. In the United States, feminism was being considered a white women's movement as it was in Australia; Black women's contributions were not being acknowledged. Black women were feeling left out. Black women felt the term 'feminism' invariably always related to being white and that it did not acknowledge Black women's fight against racism or sexism. In particular, it did not acknowledge the racism the white women's movement held against them, subconsciously or not. These arguments have been mirrored in Australia. Not only from Indigenous women but others who are not Anglo.

In 1983 I loved the way Alice Walker first coined her term 'womanism' for African American and women of colour. How I have always wanted to find such a term for Aboriginal and Torres Strait Islander women in Australia. A term that would define us in our own image and be as real and inclusive as the word Tidda. As Black women in the United States have wanted to carve out a space in these debates, so do I and others here in Australia.

It really spoke to me when Alice Walker centred Black women at the heart of the struggle, engaged with the damaging classist and racist notions of white women and their steadfast denial of Black men in the process. She never considered herself a separatist, only from time to time for her own health. I could never consider myself a separatist either. Nor could I separate from my beautiful son and the other integral males I adore in my family – the men who have always stood by and supported me in the struggle. It is about supporting and empowering them too, as they often bear the brunt of both white patriarchy and matriarchy.

So what has and hasn't changed since this book was written in 1998? Some would say nothing, a little or a lot. One could be forgiven for saying nothing, but I tend to believe it's somewhere in between. There has been some inclusion of our women in programs and policies. More collaboration with other women on a small scale rather than a wider scale. However, it is still not permeating in some areas where it should be a given. Case in point: International Women's Day every year. I have heard many stories of Black women being excluded, ignored and uninvited to events on that day. I can hear the frustration from young Black women and think, here we go again, some forty years later.

How I remember the heady early days in the 1980s when Aboriginal women were debating and taking on white women in their privileged speaking positions, and their exclusion of us. Who had the right to speak for who – 'we are women too, listen to us' were the oft-heard cries. Usually as the only Indigenous woman at their conferences, I would get howled down when I dared to challenge or express a different point of view.

The gulf and vacuum created was enormous. There were a handful of decent white women who heard, but overall it was polarising for most of them. They began arguing with each other in attack and defence of us. Of course theirs was classed as intellectual stimulation and ours as bickering and fighting among our own when we had disagreements.

Migrant women felt it too, empathised with us and seemed happy when we spoke out. During this time and to the present I have met some remarkable ethnic women who I have formed close and collaborative relationships with. Their issues were similar to ours and we spoke the same language. Here I have to mention Maria Dimopoulos, who taught me so much about diversity and migrant women. We both have been working for decades together, with varying degrees of success, to bring about a better understanding and to bring our communities closer.

Prior to this, Aboriginal women in the 1960s and 1970s were also rallying around the invisibility of our women and how the then white women's liberation movement did not take account of our racial and social issues. It seemed all too hard for them. When challenged they huffed and puffed at us and threw their arms up but provided no solutions. I still see that today when our issues are raised. Their faces get contorted and they say, 'here she goes again'. Too damn hard.

There is now a wonderful proliferation of what I have termed the 'feminisation of Aboriginal leadership' in our country. Our women are visible and leading in positions of power. The transition has proven effortless in my view and there is a greater appreciation of our men and women working together. But the expectation is that there is always gender balance in leading their community organisations.

In 2002 I was part of a three-member team to review the Aboriginal and Torres Strait Islander Commission (ATSIC). It was one of the hardest jobs I have ever done and I was furious when our report did not even get to Parliament before ATSIC was dismantled by the federal government. I had proposed equal representation for men and women in all tiers of the organisation. I was told in no uncertain terms that this would never get through and that appointments should be based on merit – even by some of the ATSIC women – but nevertheless the review committee allowed me to put in a minority report that would mandate and equalise all positions. I remember saying to my two white male colleagues, 'Well Black women will love me, not sure about the blokes.' So structurally it was a good beginning. I count this as one of my enduring legacies.

It's been a natural progression since the establishment of the National Congress of Australia's First Peoples in 2009. The Congress was set up by Indigenous Australians, had an Ethics Council and mandated equal gender representation of men and women in the organisation. It was a cultural imperative so that women's and men's business could prosper and be respected as it once was. The then Sex Discrimination Commissioner, Liz Broderick, praised this ruling and suggested that the 100 ASX bodies should implement these egalitarian measures also. Good luck, women.

Prior to this the voices of Indigenous women were denied and usually dismissed in other representative bodies that were largely masculine and misogynistic. Across the country, where leadership has been male dominated, the structures are slowly changing with our women being represented as mayors, CEOs, chairs and on boards. In fact, recently there has been a national debate raging about the respect for women and quotas for political parties. I believe this is the only way to correct an incorrect system. When the system is broken it must be fixed.

Globally, women's voices are being raised through movements such as Me Too and Let Her Speak. Despite the COVID-19 pandemic millions of protestors around the world gathered to demand Black justice through Black Lives Matter. Most unfortunately, 2021 was the 30th anniversary of the findings of the Royal Commission into Aboriginal Deaths in Custody in Australia being handed down and the majority of its recommendations have still not been addressed.

Deaths in custody continue to haunt us, sometimes at one per week. This is about the rate of domestic violence murders, if not slightly more – a worrying statistic that goes unnoticed by politicians, government and decision-makers. What does it take to get action?

How can Australians empathise with what is occurring overseas with Black Lives Matter when it is happening in our own backyards?

Aboriginal women suffer the worst because of this hideous inaction. They are the fastest growing prison population in Australia, usually imprisoned over menial offences, like the non-payment of parking tickets and other fines. Most of these women are also Mothers and Grandmothers. Mothers still cry and ache for the loss of their beloved sons and daughters.

A national women's summit is being called for around domestic and family violence and other long-neglected issues. Hopefully this will include the participation of a number of Aboriginal and Torres Strait Islander women. It has taken so long and it is no wonder we are angry and frustrated. Will they be brave enough to compare the incarceration and deaths in custody statistics of our women with the domestic and family violence statistics? Even braver, will they do something about it?

And will the government be brave enough to action June Oscar's groundbreaking *Wiyi Yani U Thangani, Women's Voices Report*, tabled in the Federal Parliament in December 2020? The report, published by the Australian Human Rights Commission, is the first time since 1986 that Aboriginal and Torres Strait Islander women and girls have been heard as a collective about our rights, strengths, challenges, and aspirations. It paints a whole-of-life picture, giving a well-overdue First Nations gender-lens on everything from housing and care work to education, governance and economic empowerment. It puts forward an ambitious plan for structural change to ensure our women are at the decision-making table when it comes to determining all aspects of our lives. We need to action this report – it is well and truly time that our voices are responded to by all Australian governments.

There are many essays in this book that were written some decades ago, and many things have changed not one iota since. There is still so much to be written about *Sister Girl* issues and I now hand the pen over to others, especially younger women, who face injustice on a daily basis. And there is much evidence that young women are taking up the baton. A generational shift is swamping our nation with articulate, educated and well thought-out arguments from strong young Black women. It is happening, folks.

Firing On in the Mind

I wanted to write about the silent history of Aboriginal women that has been the experience of so many of my Mother's and Grandmother's generation. Although we learnt about the pioneering efforts of mostly European males, little was recorded about the 'backbone' of the pastoral industry, the Aboriginal men and women who toiled as stockmen and domestic servants. This is so much a part of Australian history and it is about my history. The stories deserve recognition and need to be rescued, recorded and shared. I wrote this piece in 1987, just prior to the bicentenary.

—

In attempting to present evidence of our true situation we are furiously attacked by white Australians … going back 200 years … the past is finished! … Yet kill [our] mother, rape [our] land, psychologically attack and keep [us] in a powerless position each day – does it not fire on in the mind of the victim? Does it continue to scar and affect the thinking? Deny it, but still it exists.[1]

Is it possible for white Australians to write 'Aboriginal' history? Aboriginal history differs from white history in its concerns and perspectives and probably its methods. However, whites too are crucially a part of the process. Whites are exercising power and making decisions which affect Aboriginal lives. White norms and values are enshrined in our institutions and white knowledge and ways of valuing are taught and recorded in our schools. We are all products of history and, as a consequence, occupy particular positions of privilege or disadvantage.

Aboriginal people have been excluded from the pages of white history, and denied access to the records of their own people. There do exist, in those historical accounts of what occurred throughout Australian history, many examples of Aboriginal involvement in the blazing of trails, in the establishment of settlements, and in every area of Australian 'advancement'. However, they are hidden within the historical accounts that exist. They remain nameless men and women.

Aboriginal writing is concerned with history, with precise knowledge of the history of Aboriginal existence, gleaned if necessary from white records, and prised out of white archives. Aboriginal people did not write down their knowledge, thoughts and experiences. These were passed on, in the normal course of social life, by word of mouth, supplemented by graphic representations with regionally and socially coded and variable meanings. Circumstances changed radically as European settlement and influence spread to the farthest corners of the continent. A great deal of oral traditional material has been rescued and recorded. In a growing number of Aboriginal communities the people themselves are setting up their own literature centres where they are tape recording, transcribing and translating their stories. These centres have ensured the emergence of a written Aboriginal literature. Aboriginal people have begun to be heard by others, as they name their own world and relate their own experiences.

The difference, the advantage for Aboriginal writers, in spite of so many external difficulties, comes from the different relationships that exist between Aboriginal people and their communities, and the different role and functions of writers in relation to those communities. Aboriginal writers have a sense of purpose, an urgent task on behalf of their community.

This article examines the life experience of Aboriginal women domestics during the inter-war years of the 1920s and 1930s. Although all of the six women interviewed worked mainly in these years, it was quite a difficult task to locate the topic of their 'total life experience', it being so blurred into the general as the commonplace tends to be. However, linking up routines with the time of certain bosses, locations and their respective duties did not seem to present a problem. Having the advantage of being Black and female, I am grateful that these women confided many intimately personal things, and the narratives show that the quality and the significance of their experiences are not necessarily correlated with the recorder's educational credentials but, rather, with the rapport established between recorder and narrator and with the advanced age of the informants. However, I could not dismiss the idea that while some startling information was revealed, endless tales could be forthcoming from each of these women that could form the basis of a biography. Interviews were conducted in Brisbane in June and July 1987 with the late June Bond, Rita Huggins, Margaret Pickering and Agnes Williams from the Cherbourg Aboriginal Settlement, Daphne Lavelle from Hervey Bay and Annie Hansen from Lake Nash.

One exceptional woman, June Bond, sadly passed away in August. She inspired many people through her commitment to and staunch views on the past, present and future of Aboriginal people. A pillar of society, she raised twelve children as well as nephews and grandchildren, and will be dearly missed. It is not until Aboriginal people of such high calibre are no longer with us that one realises the urgency, enormity and value of the task which awaits us in recording and transcribing this precious information.

This point was recently raised at a Brisbane Aboriginal women's meeting in November where a recommendation was put forward to acknowledge the achievements and give credit to the efforts of our older women in appreciation of their unshakable commitment to the betterment of our community while they are still with us. This gesture would also serve as an inspiration and encouragement to younger women.

Younger women today have become more politically aware and conscious of the need to learn all we can from our Elders. By listening to their stories of hardships and years of experience, it is often considered that we are the fortunate ones, having hardly experienced the rigours of the stringent 'controls' they endured. While their presence still commands respect, it does sometimes dictate an air of conservatism due to the 'controls' under which Aboriginal people of their generation were placed.

From the end of the nineteenth century through to the 1930s, the effects of economic depression and drought, and a resulting decline in the rural economy, increased competition for employment. This, together with government policy, resulted in further relocation of Aboriginal people to reserves and missions. This effectively removed these people from the opportunity to participate in the labour force. Aboriginal women found work as domestic servants and nursemaids in station homesteads and, in some cases, as stock workers.

In Queensland, the Aborigines and Torres Strait Islanders Act of 1897 empowered the Minister, through a system of police protectors and reserve superintendents, to control the movements of Aborigines, to enter employment contracts on their behalf, to hold any funds they might have and control their spending. The Act assigned Aborigines inferior status, and regarded them as slave labour without entitlement to the wages enjoyed by their white counterparts. The real significance of the Act was its denial in law of fundamental human rights. This Act is the foundation on which all future legislation, including the current legislation, is based. In 1981 Frank Brennan sj, Adviser to the Queensland Catholic Bishops, was assigned to prepare a consultation document on the 'Services Legislation', which was to complement proposals for a system of land tenure over reserves called 'Deeds of Grant in Trust'. These are now operating on reserves, but have made very little difference to the wellbeing and self-determination of Aboriginal people. Thus, a dependency syndrome on the state government still remains.

All interviewees spoke unfavourably about the repressive Act; however, its role in the exploitation of labour is best explained by Ruby de Satgé:

> Well the Act means that if you are sitting down minding your own business, a station manager can come up to you and say, 'I want a couple of blackfellows'. He could come from any station, any property that wanted a blackfella. They just come in and take him, no asking, just take … Just like picking up a cat or a dog.[2]

When asked how this could be so, she replied, 'Simple, they just take them to the police station and their fingerprints are put on a piece of paper and they're signed on for twelve months!'[3]

The majority of women interviewed were 'under the Act', and are now respected Elders in their local Brisbane Aboriginal community. It is from their past experiences, coupled with their infinite knowledge and wisdom that they are held in the highest regard and esteem by their people. Seniority, as well as individual personality, plays a large part in determining Aboriginal women's power, which increases with age. Indeed, elderly Aboriginal people are valued because of their scarcity. Forty-three per cent of the

Aboriginal population is under 15 years of age and 17 per cent is over 40 years of age, compared with the total Australian population which is 27 per cent and 34 per cent respectively. This indicates an almost double percentage in the younger Aboriginal population and an almost halved percentage in the older population, compared with other Australians. A further breakdown of the latter statistics reveals the Aboriginal population in the 60-plus age group as only 5 per cent, compared with 13 per cent of the total Australian population.[4] As well as children, the elderly are the most prized possessions in any Aboriginal community.

Their stories depict a life of subjugation and exploitation; however, all of them have managed to retrieve their rightful and elevated positions in Aboriginal society. It seems that they have never lost their identity, strength and independence despite all the injustices and obstacles that have hindered them.

Marnie Kennedy of Palm Island died a few months before the publication of her book *Born a Half-Caste*. She addressed the domestic servant situation in this way:

> When the whites had pounded every bit of our lifestyle, culture, language and our identity out of us, which left us a mass of bruised and broken humanity, we were signed on and sent out to slave for the white man.[5]

With understandable bitterness and, surprisingly, some fondness, a complex interrelationship enmeshed Black and white in the domestic sphere. The Europeans were gripped by a racist mythology which claimed that Aboriginal people were inferior, and were poor workers who needed to be firmly controlled. The mythology demanded that Europeans treat Aboriginal people firmly but fairly, and take care that any kindness was not construed as weakness. Fear, the mythology warned, must never be shown, and white supremacy had to be upheld at all times.[6] Indeed, even today it is familiar to hear older Aboriginal people refer to people in powerful positions as 'Mr Jim', 'Miss Marjorie' or 'Boss'.

Europeans worked closely alongside Aboriginal people, needed their labour and called them 'our Aborigines'. However, Ruby de Satgé remarked:

> The white head stockman at Victoria River Downs used to work all the black boys they had like animals. He used to treat them like dirt ... I can't see them treating them any better anywhere else. It was shocking![7]

Most European children in the north were reared by Aboriginal house servants, and some were suckled at the breasts of Black wet-nurses. Aboriginal people resented the controls and poor conditions they suffered, but many grew to respect and even like their own European bosses. June Bond for instance reported most favourable attitudes between herself and her employers. In fact, she states that she was encouraged and helped by all the families she worked for, and spoke warmly of a 'wonderful atmosphere'. On the other hand, Agnes Williams related a rather gruesome story.

> You see this scar on my face, well I reckon that was done by her [the mistress] because we had to scrub the pots and pans. And you know those Steelo pads with the gold threads through them, well I went off cleaning and she came in while I was cleaning the silver and I wasn't doing it right according to her. So she got it [the Steelo] and scrubbed my face and said: 'Now this is the way you rub!' And I swear from that day till this, when I think about it, I wonder how this [scar] started. Of course now I have to wear hats all the time and keep out of the sun. [Agnes Williams has a fair complexion,

and the thing on her face developed into a form of sun cancer which is at times a bright pink.]

Thus, both Black and white held mixed feelings towards each other. Both were in a relationship of attraction and repulsion – of mutual dependence.

Within this relationship of interdependence, Aboriginal people were the powerless partners. This can be seen in the very food they were given to eat. While the Europeans on the station enjoyed butter, jam, fruit, vegetables and sometimes beer with their beef, the Aboriginal people only received bread, beef, tea and sugar, with the occasional potato.

Agnes Williams commented:

I worked for a Police Sergeant. They were English people at Killarney with three children. I was a servant and treated like shit. I had food rations and bread and dripping. The children would 'sneak' me some food at times. When we had dinner I was given scraps because according to them [the people I worked for], this is what I was used to. I was there for four years.

Ruby de Satgé said of one station: 'They fed the dogs better than they fed the blacks out there!'[8] All the Aboriginal women interviewed reported the 'scraps' which they were given to eat in an area which was segregated from the whites. Daphne Lavelle usually ate in the kitchen after the main meal was served, as did all the women, only to jump up and down when asked for the missing salt and pepper and tomato sauce. Even in the stock camp in the bush, the Europeans camped and ate apart from the Black stockmen. As Marnie Kennedy recalled, 'On some of the stations around, the darkies were made to eat outside and had their food dished out for them. They were not allowed to touch any food.'[9]

Only two interviewees were allowed to touch food, and this was only in relation to menial tasks like washing and peeling potatoes and other vegetables. They never ever handled meat or assisted with the making of food like bread and scones. This can only point to the paranoia whites had about Blacks 'contaminating' their food. Certain jobs held more status and responsibility: Annie Hansen after twenty-five years on one station, where she had witnessed two generations being raised, 'graduated' to the rank of cook.

Life as a 'worker' commenced early for Aboriginal women. As Amy Laurie explained: 'I've never been to school. My experience was on the bullock.'[10] And Margaret Pickering was only 8 years old when she began milking cows and herding cattle to make a living for her father, mother and three brothers. What she could not foretell was that twelve more brothers and sisters would follow, increasing the family size and, of course, this would mean more mouths to feed. The remaining women reported a similar story: 'At Grade 4, girls were made to leave school as it was time to go to work,' Rita Huggins said.

Domestic service was viewed in the dominant white ideology as a fitting vocation for Aboriginal women. Indeed, the offensively paternalistic relation of whites to Aboriginal people at the time is exemplified by J. W. Bleakley, who was responsible for the administration of Queensland Aborigines from 1913 to 1942.

> The increasing difficulty in obtaining white girls for domestic service had created what, at first, we regarded as a heaven-sent opportunity for native girls to secure a good home with food and clothing, and receive motherly care and domestic training: not forgetting, of course, the saving to the State of the cost of their upkeep. Many of these girls were half-castes and there should be the further advantage of the civilised home background and preparation for their assimilation into

the white community that their half-white blood entitled them to. With this in view, large numbers of these girls, many of them fresh from leaving school, some as young, even, as ten years of age (when the average white girl would still be playing dolls) had been brought to the metropolis and placed in service with employers.[11]

Simply because they were Aboriginal, they were neither expected nor allowed to rise any higher in occupational status than this; the basic though essential services they performed, for minimal returns, were never intended to bring them into economic competition with the white worker.[12]

Young Aboriginal women were taken from country reserves and missions; the majority of interviewees went to white homes that wanted maids. White women considered such help essential to the running of a household, especially in the tropics. In more isolated areas, Black women performed a wider range of jobs than their European counterparts: they mustered cattle, went droving, served as shepherds, worked at road and fence building and repairing.

When they were equipped with trousers and boots, and with calico tied around their breasts and hair, they were a match for any man, except in the throwing of beasts. They worked as hard as their men and possibly harder, since men often passed over disagreeable jobs to the women and sat back to watch them work.[13] After being asked who dug the post holes in the west, Ruby de Satgé replied:

'I did,' jokingly flexing her muscles. 'Crow bar and shovel. No machines out there. I used a brace and bit to bore the posts for the wire, too. I strained the wire with a forky stick.'[14]

Indeed the term 'houseworker' took on a broad meaning in terms of spheres of duty and space in which work was carried out. It was used to denote any person whose work was orientated towards the needs of the station family or the domestic needs of other employees, white or Black. This could include herding cattle, drawing water, butchering bullocks, cleaning; in fact, anything which was not related to stockwork or tasks outside the boundary of the main camp.[15] Marnie Kennedy reported of her miscellaneous duties at the Austin farm:

> My duties were housework, washing and ironing, taking smoko to men in the fields – helped to cut chop-chop for the horses, cut cane, helped load, lay rail lines for the cane train.
>
> The only job I hated there was having to use a flying fox to draw water from the creek. That was gut-catching work as I was only six stone.[16]

The Aboriginal women's accounts depict a long and fairly arduous day, in which they were required to perform many and varied tasks. The day went by according to a disciplined and fixed routine. All women reported a set pattern to their daily chores. Daphne Lavelle reported that the emptying of the 'piss pots' was the chore she detested the most. The Black woman's entire day seemingly revolved around catering for the white family's needs.

She also took responsibility for the care, but not the control and discipline, of the children. By this she was to clean up after the children, bath them, change and wash nappies, etc. Rita Huggins giggled as she recalled discreetly smacking her two spoilt young charges whenever the need arose. 'I could see their grumpy little faces – you know how migaloo kids sometimes are – never into sharing. Well, when they were with me, the shoe was on the other foot, because I was the "boss woman" then!'

What happened to the firstborn children of these women who were recruited to domestic service? As was Rita Huggins' own case, her daughter was left in the care of her mother. June Bond was raised from the age of 2 by her grandmother's sister whom she called 'Granny', as her mother was also a domestic whom she rarely saw except for her yearly visits back home at Christmas time. Grandmothers, Sisters and Aunts are the most frequently used persons in Aboriginal communities – the extended family plays a very important role in child care arrangements. It is very common for a member of a child's extended family, particularly the grandmother, to look after a child or children for short periods of time because the parents are unable to do so for one reason or another (in this case, employment). Sometimes these arrangements will extend for longer periods of time, to the point where the child might be identified as belonging to the person looking after him or her and be regarded as having been 'fostered', in a way.

A child growing up in an Aboriginal community is also surrounded by relatives who have particular responsibilities towards that child and who play a meaningful role in child-rearing. The care and discipline of children by the family is often extended to the wider Aboriginal community. Generally there is the feeling that children belong to everybody and, in a large gathering, children are the responsibility of all, be they female or male, young or old. Aboriginal children therefore tend to grow up in a familiar, warm world of the Aboriginal family and community and, generally, children are the responsibility of the entire family rather than of the biological parents alone.

The Master and Servant Act of 1845 was a feudal piece of legislation which made it an offence for employees to leave their place of employment without permission. Agnes Williams reported on how she was treated:

When they went away at weekends, say every six weeks, to see their son in Toowoomba, they used to lock me in a cell.

What could I do? I couldn't run away as I had no money and nowhere to go.

The Act was fully exploited by unscrupulous employers and workers who 'absconded' were hunted, captured and punished. The police were generally willing to use force against Aboriginal people, even though many of them were also officially Aboriginal protectors. They tracked down runaway workers and brought them back to face a thrashing or prison for absconding from a work contract.[17] The reality of this is best brought home by Marnie Kennedy:

> Aborigines were not allowed to leave their jobs if they wanted to or their boss was cruel to them. We were to do our job be it right or wrong. If we were signed on for twelve months, then we had to do twelve months, however much we hated it. We were not free to go anywhere outside our employment.[18]

Aboriginal domestics worked long hours, in most cases a fifteen-hour day; and there were no holidays and leisure activity was minimal, even on Sundays. These young women became very homesick on occasions; not only because of their relative youthfulness but because for most it was their first time away from home and family. Marnie Kennedy had a 'yearning' to see her mother but had to get a permit, while Agnes Williams was not permitted to return home on compassionate grounds for her mother's funeral, an event she regrets with understandable bitterness and hatred to this day. In fact, many of her family ostracised her for her failure to attend:

> I wasn't even allowed to go home for my Mother's funeral because according to him [the master], because my mother and father were separated and my Grandmother reared me up, that he didn't see any reason for me to go home.

My father never spoke to me for years after that. I was 15 at the time, my Mother was only in her 30s when she died.

To Aboriginal people, the deep, religious and spiritual significance of funerals places a huge onus on relatives and friends to attend these important events. A funeral is also viewed as paying final respects to a worthy and cherished person. No matter whether the deceased is a close relative or community acquaintance, attendance is commanded. Since it is one of the most honoured etiquettes of Aboriginal society, attendance may number in the hundreds. Absence at an Aboriginal funeral does not go unnoticed, particularly if it is that of a close relative. Non-attendance, therefore, is generally scorned and considered a grave insult to the deceased and all surviving relatives.

White employers also often complained of the Aboriginal women's need for constant supervision. Mrs Gilruth, wife of the Northern Territory Administrator, wrote in a newspaper article:

The lubra can be made a good domestic and is perfectly willing to learn … but black women are not self reliant. They could not be left in charge of the house of children, but if anyone is over them they are alright.[19]

Aboriginal women could be continually checked as to their thoroughness. However, as Karen Flick so adequately summed up, 'The white people choose the employment system and we are dominated by white opinion and white prejudices and white standards.'[20]

Agnes Williams believed that her female bosses were the worst masters, and even more dictatorial than the males. She commented, 'You know, the women were worse than the men in the way in which they treated you.'

Despite the predominance of patriarchal rule in Australian society,

Australia was colonised on a racially imperialistic base and not on a sexually imperialistic base. No degree of patriarchal bonding between white male colonisers and Aboriginal men overshadowed white racial imperialism. In fact, white racial imperialist ideology granted all white women, however victimised by sexist oppression, the right to assume the role of oppressor in relation to Black men and Black women.

In the colonial context, the Black man had virtually lost his bargaining powers and the coloniser assumed almost total control; hence, the interaction between white man and Black woman was one marked by compulsion. Often young Aboriginal women lived almost simultaneously with her Aboriginal husband and a white man who, in practice, had more rights over her than her husband because of the great discrepancy between them in status.

The patriarchal nature of contemporary society means that Aboriginal women were subject to further specific oppression by both Aboriginal and white men. They have been typecast as capable only of roles and deserving only of treatment deemed unworthy or undesirable for that more highly valued, rarer 'commodity' – the white woman.[21] Male dominance was, and is, a major ingredient in the culture Europeans brought with them to Australia. This message came through to Aboriginal people, directly or indirectly, in words and deeds, in almost all their contacts with Europeans.

The main thing that could destroy Aboriginal women's relationships with white women would be their sexual relations with white employers. It is reported that in the Northern Territory, on completing the day's work, some Aboriginal women visited the station house to engage in sex with the manager or other whites. Agnes Williams commented, 'From my experience all the masters wanted to do was to jump into bed with you. I told one wife after being propositioned and she didn't believe me.'

Bushmen often boasted that they preferred to employ females because they 'would work all day in the saddle and all night in the swag.'[22] Indulging in sex with Aboriginal women was a major pastime of Territory men from all ranks, including the policemen who were appointed as 'Protectors of Aborigines'.

Male chauvinism and racism underpinned the attitudes of most European men in the Territory. Bill Harney, who knew the north as well as anyone, said that there were two kinds of single men in the Territory: 'those who have lived with native women and admit it, and those who will not admit it'.[23] Many whites claimed that they were lured to the north by adventure, money – and Aboriginal women. The old Territory joke was that Europeans were 'sexplorers' who sought the joys of 'Black velvet'. Marnie Kennedy reinforced this: 'We must obey, work hard, do as we are told and be used in any way the white man wishes. White man had a few names he would call us such as "gins" and "lubra" and when he wanted a bit of lovin' we were "black velvet".'[24]

Furthermore, the men frequently saw the necessity to conquer the women as an integral part of their colonial adventure. Aboriginal women probably suffered the worst abuse at the hands of their European bosses. Sexual oppression has always gone hand in hand with conquest and exploitation, and it was perhaps inevitable on the north Australian frontier where the rough-and-tumble European adventurers came without their own women.[25] 'White men seen with peculiar frequency lusting after the black female flesh of a people they continue to hold in contempt are granted a curious lust which needs must be satisfied.'[26]

On the other hand, I believe that the concept of Aboriginal women's power in relation to sexual exploitation has never received adequate attention from anthropologists, sociologists and historians to ascertain satisfactory reasons and motivations for the Aboriginal women's position. This area certainly remains an enigma, and detailed research is required to explore the question of whether they were 'victims', or 'collaborators', or 'somewhere in between', and what, if anything, did they get out of it? Unfortunately my curiosity has never been satisfied by the social scientists.

Aboriginal women experienced the added burden of sexual exploitation based on a white male assumption of superiority over both women and Aboriginal people. In Aboriginal culture, rapists were often punished; in white society, there was nowhere Aboriginal women could turn for protection. White men controlled the law, the police, courts, government, church and prisons. Aboriginal women were in a position of utter powerlessness.

Sexual harrassment was common, too, in domestic service. As Rita Huggins explained, 'Because they [the masters] had the right to our services they believed that this had excused them to attempt to use our bodies too.'

Indeed, Archibald Meston wrote: 'The Aboriginal women are usually at the mercy of anybody, from the proprietor or manager to the stockman, cook, rouseabout and jackaroo. Frequently the women do all the housework and are locked up at night.'[27]

In most cases, the interviewees were open about this. However, it was interesting to note that the fairer-skinned women had been propositioned twice as much as their darker counterparts.

In May 1910, an article in the Brisbane *Daily Mail*, entitled 'The Aboriginal Girl – Some of her Good Points', praised Aboriginal domestics as 'household treasures' and said that there were 'three grades of girls'. It stated that there were, first, the full-blood Blacks, excellent in scullery work and any rougher duties. Then there were the older 'half-castes' who were taking up other aspects of household cleaning. Third, there were younger girls, most of them 'half-' or 'quarter-castes', who were considered to make the most patient and reliable nurses. The latter were in constant demand and could not be obtained without considerable waiting.[28]

At this time, the obsession with racial purity and prestige made any sexual relations between Black and white horrifying; however, male miscegenation through white male/Black female sexual liaisons could not upset the white sexual dominance or its economic, social and political power because the character of the social scale was determined by the white male.[29] As Sam Geary says to Hugh Watt in Katharine Susannah Prichard's novel *Coonardoo*:

'You're one of these god-damned young heroes. No "black velvet" for you, I suppose?'

'I'm going to marry white and stick white,' Hugh said.

'Oh you are, are you?' he jeered. 'Well I'll bet you a saddle you take a gin before a twelve month's out – if ever you're in this country on your own.'[30]

The opponents of miscegenation destructively argued for the segregation of 'full-bloods' and 'half-castes', completely disregarding family structures and kinship bonds. In separate settlements, the 'half-castes' – the term used to cover all people of mixed race – would be trained and educated to a basic standard and made fit to be absorbed into the white community, but at the lowest economic and social level. The men would be suitable farm or station labourers, the women would become domestic servants.[31]

Biological racist definitions such as 'half-caste', 'quarter-caste' and 'part-Aboriginal' have widely been used by whites as a divide-and-rule tactic to insist that these groups are not 'full-blooded', and that their 'white' blood is the only acceptable part that they can deal with. Aboriginal children of mixed race, primarily of Anglo-Saxon heritage, were considered more educable than their darker counterparts and were judged, therefore, to assimilate more rapidly into white society.

However, in Aboriginal society skin colour has little to do with the inner cultural principles that guide Aboriginal people. Providing that Aboriginal people show genuine commitment and active participation in their own community affairs, their degree of colour is irrelevant. For Aboriginal people, emotional scars do not necessarily have to match darkness of skin, nor does lightness indicate a lessening of knowledge of, or lack of belief in, Aboriginal culture.

Employing Black women as domestics was also a way of obtaining cheap labour under the guise of 'education'. All interviewees reported no assistance whatsoever by a helpful 'minder' in improving their literacy and numeracy skills during their periods of service. While some regularly kept in touch with family via letters which maintained their literacy skills, there were never any opportunities to strengthen these through reading or extra tuition, since domestic work totally encompassed their daily sphere. In terms of literacy, Aboriginal women were more proficient than the men, who showed more conservatism in relation to new skills.[32]

During the nineteenth century, it was common for employers to pay Aboriginal workers in kind by the provision of rations, blankets and other goods rather than by payment in cash. By the 1920s, cash payment had become common for seasonal or casual work, although often not at the same time as for other workers. In the Northern Territory only, drovers and 'half-caste apprentices' generally received a few shillings in wages: other employees were fed and clothed in return for their labours and, on most stations, a certain number of their close relations were also provided with weekly rations.[33] The Aboriginal workers were often caught in vicious cycles. For instance, to keep costs down they were only given one issue of clothing at a time from the station store.

In Queensland, it was different. There Aboriginal people, as defined in legislation, were rounded up and moved to reserves under the control of police protectors, or to missions, and systems of contract of service and payment to the then Department of Native Affairs evolved. In addition to food and shelter, Aboriginal workers under the Aboriginal Acts were supposed to receive a wage (though the amount was undefined). However, many never received a penny. As Amy Laurie reported, 'In those days we never got nothing – no wages. You know that day coloured people can't get paid or something like that. Some blokes, the white man, got paid. But I never got no money out of it.'[34]

Ruby de Satgé added:

Harry Spencer got a pair of trousers, a shirt and a pair of boots whenever he needed them. That's all the pay the men used to get. Women got a dress every six weeks – if they were lucky. The older ones got a bit of rations. They'd come down, once a week, and they'd get a little bit of flour, and a sort of handkerchief with a bit of tea and sugar tied in the corner.[35]

Even the meagre wages due to these Aboriginal workers were often withheld. Under the Act there were considerable powers vested in reserve managers to direct employment, or to direct cessation of employment, of Blacks. The remuneration required to be paid to those employed off reserves, other than those under an award, was very low.[36] As Protector of Aborigines, the superintendent looked after the departmental savings' bank accounts of residents, and regulated their use of earnings. In defending the right to withhold wages, J. W. Bleakley paternalistically stated:

Many otherwise honest employers wanted the natives to keep their earnings, however the results were often disastrous. Mostly, they arrived back at the Settlement with nothing to show for months work. In one amusing incident, after an employer handed over all wages on leaving to four natives, all were found drunk and incapable … and placed in the lock-up. Much later the natives were beginning to understand better the aims of the administration, whose officers were endeavouring to help them and protect their interests.[37]

The policy of absorbing Aboriginal people into the labour market had had a trial for twenty years, he added, and had contributed to the continued 'physical and moral degeneration' of most of his charges.[38]

A breakdown of wages earned by the interviewees was as follows:

June Bond:	6 pence per week pocket money. In 1944 when she married, she received a postal note for 8 pounds 6 pence outstanding amount for 1937–1944.
Annie Hansen:	nil, only subsistence till wages came in.
Daphne Lavelle:	10 shillings per week which she could keep as she was not under the Act.
Margaret Pickering:	2 shillings pocket money out of 10 shillings. Balance went to DNA.
Agnes Williams:	as above. After ten years' service, she received 9 pounds and 5 pence when she married.
Rita Huggins:	as above.

Clothes were a popular item to spend 'pocket money' on and, indeed, prompted June Bond's desire to work. She used to watch the 'older girls' return to the mission clad in beautiful clothes, and looked forward to the time that she could 'dress up' and afford such lavish outfits. Her mistress would send away to stores in Brisbane such as Briggs and David Jones for dresses. Daphne Lavelle, Agnes Williams and Rita Huggins also spoke glowingly of the dresses they could now afford to buy. Other items purchased were shirts, trousers, elastic-sided boots, hats, blankets and swags.

Perhaps the following extract from Willie Thaiday's *Under the Act* best summarises the exploitation of Blacks in Queensland:

> I was elected to the first Palm Island Council. We got no wages for it … We work a long time for tobacco … We try to get some kind of wages …
>
> The superintendent say, 'Well, I don't know. You know you boys been here in settlement a long time. I don't think the government will give it to you. You got tucker, and got flour, you got rice, just like wages.'
>
> We wrote to Director DNA and he came to Palm. 'Why you want wages?' He say, 'You work long time for tobacco. What you want wages for?' We say: 'We all want money, want to see what we working for.' He say: 'Give you four shillings, every fortnight.' We glad and happy too.[39]

Employers were relieved of paying a portion of the necessary means of subsistence and, hence, acquired labour power at a cost below its value. While the employer, where labour was resident, provided most of the immediate sustenance not only of employees but also of the community as a whole, this was more than offset by the fact that Aboriginal people were excluded from pastoral awards until 1965/68, that the community continued to provide some of its sustenance by traditional methods, and that, until recently, neither the employer nor the state paid any 'indirect' wages (unemployment payments, family allowances, education, health, etc.) and nearly all 'social security' functions were performed by the Aboriginal communities themselves.[40]

Aboriginal people were forced to enter into an unequal exploitative symbiosis with employers and pastoralists. Throughout the 1930s, humanitarians, unionists, missionaries and anthropologists had agitated for reforms in Aboriginal affairs. Public awareness was aroused by these groups with the aid of their mouthpieces such as the *Aborigines' Protector*, the bulletin of the Aborigines Friends' Association, and local and southern newspapers. There were calls from all of these groups for some form of organised inspection and control of the conditions of Aboriginal people employed in the pastoral industry.[41]

Matt Thomas was a unionist who had campaigned on such issues as the exploitation of Aboriginal women on road work in the Wave Hill and Victoria River Downs districts. In early 1938, he called for improved health care for station Aboriginal people, and he wrote in the southern and local press on the topic of white unemployment and the Aboriginal cause, claiming that he was unable to obtain work because of his activist stance. In August, it was reported that he was accidentally killed when he jumped onto the road about 11.40 pm, with his hand signalling for a car to stop.[42]

The North Australian Workers' Union had also exposed other cases of exploitation of Aboriginal people on stations in the late 1920s and intermittently throughout the 1930s. Because Aboriginal people were paid in rations and allocated only a few items of clothing and other necessities, the unionists classed their work as 'slave labour'.[43] Perceptively, Ray Evans draws an analogy between Aboriginal labour patterns and slavery: 'For Aboriginal workers themselves, the daily realities of their work-experience as an internally colonised people seared into the consciousness. Though rarely articulated within earshot of whites, powerlessness and alienation were as keenly felt as the deprivation of rations or the boot and the whip of their employers.'[44]

Kay Saunders further argues:

Ultimately the Blacks lost control and ownership of their vital land, and in many areas, where pastoralism replaced the traditional mode of production, they were forced to work for their conquerors. Their status resembled that of slaves, though they lacked what moderate protection the investment of capital in human resources conferred upon chattels in other societies.[45]

While domestic servants were in a situation of quasi-slavery, it is, however, important to stress the strength of Aboriginal women. Aboriginal women have always enjoyed a very large measure of personal authority, personal responsibility and personal independence, and have been able to fend for ourselves and our children despite the odds against us. Today, while many white women have won their fight to get out of their kitchens, Black women are still fighting to get in, but this time tailored to their own specifications.

Ann McGrath summarises the importance of Black women's voices being heard more clearly: 'When Aboriginal women begin to narrate their own history, we must listen intently. For then a richer understanding of their reactions and also the mechanisms they evolved to cope with their subordination will emerge.'[46]

All interviewees conveyed a sense that their time working as domestics was something of a vacuum, an 'apprenticeship' if you like, where they experienced interactions with whites who were in positions of relative power. When asked if their experience had taught them anything for their later life, they all replied 'yes' in very spontaneous ways, and added that it gave greater depth to life. Margaret Pickering believed it allowed her to mix at a very young age with whites – thus getting to know their customs. Annie Hansen learnt how to 'live like a migaloo', while Rita Huggins believed that her experience taught her to be a better housewife. They happily or unhappily accepted their lot, and recognised an Aboriginal 'worldview' based on common experience.

This article has been largely based on 'oral literature', which has been its central source. A new phenomenon of contemporary

Aboriginal writing is emerging whereby women writers have the double advantage of relating their history in literally black and white terms, and simultaneously transcending and cutting across cultural boundaries. Consequently their stories will add to the small but growing number of Aboriginal publications.

Wedmedi* – If Only You Knew

Anger when used constructively is one of my best motivations. Each time when I thought of the white feminist movement I became incensed about their exclusion of Black women, knowingly or subconsciously. One of my main sounding boards was in fact a white feminist and the mother of an Aboriginal girl. Kate Harvey is the woman I would attribute this piece to. For it was Kate who believed in my brand of feminist politics and knew that a response to the dominant kind was well overdue and necessary. We would talk for hours about the messages and feelings that I wanted established without being over-emotional. I consider this article (written in 1990) to be one of the strongest works that I have ever written.

———

As women we have all been subject to divide-and-rule socialisation, and racist and sexist ideologies. However, the overwhelming evidence and the experience of Aboriginal women points to the fact that Aboriginal women remain discriminated against due to their race rather than their gender. For example, a cosmetically apparent Aboriginal woman is regularly stereotyped on the basis of being a boong, coon, nigger, gin or abo far in excess of being a 'woman'.

---

*   Wedmedi – white woman

The lack of recognition and real understanding of this political difference is a major issue still to be resolved by the white women's movement.

Aboriginal women fight not only the material but also the cultural pressures which have sought to construct them according to someone else's mould. Western theory, language, academia – to name a few – are foreign constructs in which Aboriginal women do not fit. Therefore an oppressive society controls and manipulates Aboriginal women and in turn dictates how they should behave, think, learn, speak, write, etcetera. White feminism and women's studies are white cultural products which have been guilty of all of the above. With this in mind, much of the following will be written in Aboriginal terms of reference – a genre which like full-blown bourgeois intellectualism may tend to alienate the readership of 'others'. This style is used deliberately as the author's political statement and preference in order to elevate the powerless and to negate the superiority of the powerful.

To analyse the relationship between Aboriginal women and white feminists it is necessary to look at the history of contact between these two quite distinct political groups. In the late 1950s and 1960s, much of the Aboriginal movement's focus shifted to the national level and links were made between Aboriginal women in many states through bodies like the Federal Council of Aborigines and Torres Strait Islanders (FCAATSI) and the One People of Australia League (OPAL), during the campaigns to change the Federal Constitution and end the assimilationist denial of Aboriginal culture. This campaign, in which Aboriginal women played vital political roles, had a great moral victory in the 1967 Referendum, from which time Aborigines have been included in the national census and the Commonwealth has assumed responsibility for Aboriginal affairs. Aboriginal pressure then intensified to turn this into a real commitment in terms of new policies and particularly land rights, and so the Aboriginal movement was a very obvious element on the political scene by the early 1970s.

It was under these circumstances that the emerging Women's Liberation Movement met the Aboriginal movement. In their enthusiasm to be anti-racist, white women simply invited Aboriginal women to join their movement, with little apparent recognition of the full horror of racism in Australia, nor of how it continued to damage Aboriginal men as well as women. In asking Aboriginal women to stand apart from Aboriginal men, the white women's movement was, perhaps unconsciously, repeating the attempts made over decades by welfare administrations to separate Aboriginal women and use them against their communities. While there were Aboriginal women who were deeply aware of the politics of sexism, many reacted with anger at the limited awareness of racism shown by the white women's movement.[1]

Aboriginal women insisted that the Women's Liberation Movement recognise that the conditions they faced were different. The white women's movement argued, for example, that compared with men, women in Australia were poorly educated and worked in poorly paid jobs. Yet Aboriginal women were better educated than Aboriginal men, and when they were able to be employed, they worked in better status jobs than Aboriginal men. The white women's movement was at that time concerned with sexuality and the right to say 'yes', to be sexually active without condemnation. For Aboriginal women, who were fighting denigratory sexual stereotypes and exploitation by white men, the issue was more often the right to say 'no'. Where white women's demands to control their fertility were related to contraception and abortion, Aboriginal women were subject to unwanted sterilisation and continued to struggle against the loss of their children to interventionist welfare agencies. While Aboriginal women insisted on their right to have access to full medical services, including information about contraception, their demands to control their own fertility were related to the right to have as many children as they wanted.[2]

The Women's Liberation Movement learnt such lessons slowly and somewhat painfully, as it grappled with issues of class and race over the next two decades. A more diverse and complex white women's movement has continued a relationship with Aboriginal women which at times has been tense and distant, but at other times has allowed close personal support and productive organisational alliances.[3] Tensions persist, however, because Aboriginals are still concerned that the white women's movement does not appreciate how racism shapes sexism, nor the needs of Aboriginal women to be supported in strengthening their whole community and ensuring their children's futures.[4]

Australian historiography has been notably silent about relationships between white women and Black women and, in particular, female employers and their Aboriginal servants. It is imperative that any discussion of race and gender includes the issue of oppression of Black women by white women, however. Indeed, given the effort devoted to feminist consciousness raising and the question of exposing oppression of women by men, it is ironic that white women have usually excluded such a critical analysis from their purview. In white feminist writings, a wall of silence invariably has been maintained on this issue. The focus has been on 'women' as an entity as constituting the oppressed. Yet this literature has never raised the question of whether women themselves are oppressors. Instead, there has been a tendency to equate the situation of white women with that of all women. When the complex factors of race and gender are considered, however, white women's activities have to be seen as part of the colonisation and oppression of Black women. Certainly, sisterhood was not powerful enough to transcend such racial boundaries.

There is a growing body of evidence which describes how Black women were treated by their white counterparts. In several recent works, Aboriginal women authors have begun to expose the gross inequality of female interrelationships, and the dynamics of the oppression of Black by white. Such oppression was most pronounced in the domestic servant sphere. When Aboriginal girls and women were sent into domestic service, they found that the 'boss' was almost invariably a female. White female employers also designated their white domestics as unequal, but Black workers were held in even lower regard. At times, close bonds did develop between white and Black women, but the boundaries of the unequal relationship were clearly defined by the former along the lines of class and race. Furthermore, in many situations Aboriginal women were subject to quite brutal treatment by white women.

Clearly the issue of oppression of Black women by white women is a contentious one, requiring far more attention in the future. Yet the work of Black writers and their experiences illustrate that race and gender relations cannot be considered in isolation, one from the other. Myrna Tonkinson observes:

The virtual absence of friendship between Black and White women in colonial Australia, at the same time as sexual relationships between Black women and White men were widespread, is an apparent paradox. Yet, it makes sense in the logic of colonial relations. In all colonial relations there is an assumption by the colonisers that they are inherently superior to the colonised … Since friendship is founded on notions of affinity and equality between individuals, it is not a condition to which colonial settings are conducive.[5]

These comments about the colonial era are still relevant today. White feminists' continued attempts to impose their politics onto Aboriginal women despite Aboriginal women's clear rejection is most certainly an attempt at intellectual colonisation.

Aside from the domestic servant sphere, the oppression of Aboriginal women and children by white women was also extreme in the fields of welfare and education and this situation continues today. Many Aboriginal children have suffered brutally at the hands of white women who have always known what is 'best' for these children. White women were and are still a major force in the implementation of government policies of assimilation and cultural genocide. As welfare workers, institution staff, school teachers and adoptive/foster mothers, white women continue to play major oppressive roles in the lives of Aboriginal women and children.

Racism in the welfare and education systems continues to be a major focus of Aboriginal women's political struggles. These are the issues which Aboriginal women activists see as priorities rather than those taken up by white feminists. The stealing of Aboriginal children is one of the greatest political concerns of Aboriginal women today. Unfortunately, it has too often been white women responsible for tearing Black children from their mothers' arms and placing them in the care of other white women who often abused them. While this practice is allowed to continue there can be no peace or true political alliances between Black and white women in this country.

It is no excuse to say that white women are not the ones who make the oppressive government policies, as they have played crucial roles in the support and implementation of these policies, in both paid and unpaid capacities. In this sense, white women cannot be seen as powerless in the face of male power, as they are in fact collaborators in the use of white (male) power against Black people. When Aboriginal women, either as mothers or community workers or political activists, challenge the racist abuse of their children, they too often find themselves struggling against a white woman who is defending individual or institutional racism. Generally, Black women feel no sense of relief to find that they are dealing with a white woman instead of a white man in these matters. Many say they prefer to deal with white men because they then escape the missionary-style zeal that some feminists employ in their belief that because they are feminists they are experts on *all* and that Aboriginal women need 'raising up' to their level of feminist consciousness. And so we see that colonialism is alive and well in the women's movement. Some feminists behave just like the missionaries' wives who wanted to raise Aboriginal women to the lofty heights of white women's sex roles and Christianity, too arrogant to realise that Aboriginal women's traditional social, political and spiritual roles gave them a far better position than white women could ever imagine.

White feminists, generally using middle-class privileges, have successfully challenged the male power structures of governments and now have significant input into policies and practices affecting women and girls. It is vital that they also challenge their own inherent racism, both individually and collectively, in analysis, policy and practice. Otherwise, as white women become empowered through the women's movement, their roles as oppressors of Aboriginal women and children will be multiplied and reinforced rather than dismantled. Aboriginal women may therefore find themselves more opposed to white women than previously. The increasingly powerful role of femocrats in government structures opens up areas where white women might share with Aboriginal women the benefits gained through the women's movement – if Aboriginal women's demands are respected and the politics of difference are understood. These possibilities are clearly evident in the fields of education and welfare policy development. However, given white women's general lack of analysis and real *understanding* of racism, both within the movement and in society in general, Aboriginal women continue to be extremely sceptical that 'sisterhood is powerful' in a *positive* sense in relation to white women. It seems we are still saying 'sisterhood might be powerful' in a positive sense. So far, white women have been very powerful in relation to Aboriginal women – unfortunately, in an unforgettably and at times overwhelmingly negative sense.

The politics of representation is another matter of concern for Aboriginal women which white women do not consider important enough to come to terms with. Aboriginal women's demand that they have the right to choose their own representatives in interactions with the women's movement is still opposed by some white feminists. White women do not appreciate the group cohesiveness and communal nature of relationships inherent in Aboriginal society: the connectedness which determines who actually does what, who has responsibility for what, who takes responsibility for saying things to whom, who does the saying, who does the writing. Women's position in Aboriginal culture, both traditional and contemporary, situates them within a powerful network of female support. This means that Aboriginal women put into practice the ideal which white feminists refer to as 'sisterhood' – a concept feminists borrowed from the Black civil rights movement in America and yet to be fully understood by white women who still suffer the legacy of a patriarchal culture which divides them.

This powerful relationship between Aboriginal women has been practised since the Dreaming. It has been absolutely vital to the Aboriginal struggle to survive the attempted genocide since the invasion and certainly will not be done away with for the sake of protecting white feminism! Some white women display a complete lack of respect for Aboriginal women's cultural values and political structures in their attempts to create divisions between Black women to serve the purpose of their tokenism. Despite this, Aboriginal women's unity remains strong at community, state and national levels, reinforced by the need to stand united against any form of racism.

White women do like to decorate their audiences with a few Black faces, exploiting Aboriginal women to protect themselves against charges of eurocentrism, but this only amounts to a special brand of feminist tokenism. When it comes to who represents Aboriginal women, an easy and accessible option for white women is to ignore (even after they have been directed about) these necessary structures which Aboriginals have established in order to protect themselves against an ignorant and racist audience. Instead, feminists tend to recruit Black women whom they acknowledge as 'safe', uncritical and hopefully espousing their ideals of womanhood and sisterhood. This practice reinforces white supremacy and is one of the lowest forms of maternalism.

On top of this, some white feminists still continue the racist practice of supporting white 'experts' to speak and write about Aboriginal women, thus maintaining their role of misinterpreting and misappropriating Aboriginal women's culture and history and undermining their politics. This practice reinforces the exploitative roles of 'expert' from the dominant colonising culture and 'subject' from the colonised and oppressed group. Aboriginal people would probably be one of the most researched groups on earth. Anthropologists, sociologists, criminologists and historians are some of the social scientists who have attempted to unravel the milieu of Aboriginal existence in Australia. Male anthropologists who entered the field failed to recognise that their work operated within the limitations of their own gender biases as well as the gender restrictions within Aboriginal and Torres Strait Islander societies. White female researchers also operate within certain limitations and expectations relating to both indigenous cultures and their own cultural realm. Black women are acutely aware of this and do not welcome uncredentialled researchers into their lives, as much information has been misconstrued, abused and misused by unscrupulous people irrespective of gender.

White women's attempts to silence or control Aboriginal challenges to the inherent racism in feminist theory and practice of course serve to reinforce Aboriginal women's criticism that white feminists still do not recognise their own racism. White women are still not prepared to step outside their culturally determined frameworks or forgo their privileged positions as part of the dominant culture. Unfortunately, some recent interactions between Black women and radical feminists have only increased the Aboriginal community's feelings of anger at the women's movement, reinforcing the sense of alienation which serves to drive the wedge further in what was already a tenuous relationship. While white feminist theory may espouse the *ideals* of sisterhood and solidarity, feminist practice continues to damage the possibility that this rhetoric could be translated into *action*.

What white women do not realise is that, despite the general diversity of opinions in Aboriginal society, the strong stance that Aboriginal women take against the white women's movement remains universal. There has not been in Australia to date one published document by an Aboriginal or Torres Strait Islander woman who avidly supports the women's liberation movement. There is certainly no discussion of support for it in Aboriginal community circles.

The commonality of views about the movement has led Aboriginal women to participate in inquisitively piecemeal ways at white women's conferences but to become detached and again placed on the peripheries when challenges are made to a eurocentric agenda, or to insensitive and offensive content matter. Or they become excluded due to some valid concerns or goals which white feminists often overlook, for example creating a space for Indigenous women to speak together, either in sessions or with other women. Another goal would be to explore racism and its centrality to Aboriginal women's lives.

When attending these gatherings Aboriginal women are usually seen in several limited and oppressive ways. Foremostly tokenistic, if we are at all articulate then we are exceptional, assimilated – too white to be Black and too Black to be white – sharing and participating in white beliefs and values. Or we are seen as angry, hostile, threatening, and subversive to white women's interests, agendas and goals.

These perverse perceptions indicate that white women continue to regard Aboriginal women as inferior to them and will therefore insist on treating Black women accordingly. Due to ingrained racism, Black women are not respected as women because of the temporary amnesia that persists, obscuring that we are, in fact, women too and not just Blacks. Black women experience a series of multiple, simultaneous oppressions continuously.

Until there is a real understanding of racism in this country and genuine moves made towards racial equality, many Aboriginal women will not be prepared to talk publicly, to audiences of 'others', about the oppression they suffer through sexism. White feminists' interference in this issue is unwelcome, as to date it has only reinforced racist stereotypes of Aboriginal women, men and culture. However, in the meantime white women should not forget that they do not exclusively 'own' feminism.

The often pathetic excuses given when Aboriginal women are not in attendance at women's conferences are that 'we don't know of any who would be interested', 'no one came even though they were invited', and 'the Black American and Maori women are really into theoretical debates in their countries, why aren't the Aboriginal women here in Australia?' Well, perhaps they're just too smart to enter into yet another alien discourse and institution designed by and for whites without any consultation with Black people in the first place, a process which would simply repeat the whole history of Black/white relations since the invasion of this land.

It is also apparent that Aboriginal women are viewed as the 'other' based on a menial or sexual image: as more sensual but less cerebral, more interesting perhaps but less intellectual, more passive but less critical, more emotional but less analytical, more exotic but less articulate, more withdrawn but less direct, more cultured but less stimulating, more oppressed but less political.

Aboriginal women will always be on the margins and will consider it an unnecessary and irrelevant social movement in which their voices will never be heard. The white women's movement in Australia needs to implement some revolutionary zeal which overcomes oppression *per se* so that all women may benefit.

Aboriginal women are not prepared to engage in discussions with white women until meaningful and anti-racist discourses are constructed which transcend the barriers that separate us. At present Aboriginal women's experiences with white feminists prevent them from seeing dialogue as anything but a naive and tokenistic beginning, as race is finally surfacing on the agenda but is yet to be understood. On those occasions when there is collaboration between white and Black women, meaningful representations and negotiations with mentally and spiritually evolved white individuals or groups must occur in order to empower Aboriginal women and to address their concerns. This might then mean that white feminists become part of the solution instead of part of the problem.

Writing My Mother's Life

Probably good therapy after one writes a book is to reflect on why one wrote it! It can show the absolute importance for a writer to have written what she or he considers to be 'the right message'. Taking time to reflect on why it was essential to write a book about my Mother helped me understand the enormity of her compassion and love toward her fellow human beings. While I knew she was a product of her time, as am I, the challenge to encapsulate the generational and social mores and political ideologies without tampering any further with our mother/daughter relationship is set out in this essay written in 1991.

—

In attempting to provide an analysis of writing my Mother's life, it is necessary first to elucidate the vital role oral history plays in the recording of Aboriginal stories and how it has changed over the years. Oral history is a specific method of recording people's recollections of past events. Aboriginal people did not write down their knowledge, thoughts and experiences. These were passed on in the normal course of social life, by word of mouth supplemented by graphic representations with regionally and socially coded and variable meanings. Circumstances changed radically as European settlement and influence spread to the farthest corners of the continent. Fortunately, a great deal of oral history material has been rescued and recorded.

The linguistic habits of Aboriginal communities which survived colonisation have changed along with their lifestyles, more or less drastically according to the length and nature of the non-Aboriginal presence. The continuing oral transmission of most Aboriginal vernacular literature is threatened by social changes, despite the renewed commitment of some communities to their languages today.[1]

Since the advent of tape recorders, one is able to capture information from people and document it as it is told from personal accounts and experiences. In the past, oral history has been largely ignored by historians, so the other side of the written account has been missing. Had Aboriginals been interviewed during the mission and government reserve period, for example, their accounts would have been entirely different from those written by missionaries to their church societies and by administrators in their annual reports to the government.

When looking at the history of a particular reserve or mission – in this case Cherbourg – it is necessary to examine government documents and annual reports pertaining to that particular place. When reading these sources, it is important to remember that the reports by administrators were frequently inaccurate and were often in conflict with Aboriginal statements about certain events and incidents.

In order to interpret history from an Aboriginal point of view it is necessary to read between the lines of those government documents and reports. The reports are housed in the Queensland Department of Community Services, previously known as the Department of Aboriginal and Islander Advancement and, before that, the Department of Native Affairs. All these departments recorded enormous amounts of information about the Aboriginals and Torres Strait Islanders they knowingly oppressed.

In the 1920s, the Queensland government pushed tribes out of their traditional areas and placed them onto mission stations and government reserves, allegedly to protect them from whites but in reality to place them under the control of missionaries and government officials. This became the isolation and control period, when Aboriginal people were deliberately and systematically cut off from their traditional way of life and forced to conform to a European lifestyle. It was during this period that written work was first introduced.

This commenced the fragmentation of oral Aboriginal tradition. Traditional customs and practices – such as language, corroborees, ceremonies, religious beliefs and marriage laws – were strongly discouraged and condemned by missionaries and managers. They saw Aboriginal customs and practices as being undesirable aspects of a heathen culture, and set about trying to change Aboriginal people. When they considered that this change had been achieved, the Queensland government introduced new policies of absorption and assimilation, aimed at replacing the former policy of protection and forcing Aboriginal people away from reserves into the white community.

Ever since these forced movements, first from traditional areas in the 1920s and then from isolated communities in the 1940s and 1950s, Aboriginal people have become more dispersed into rural towns and cities, and this has resulted in the further fragmentation of Aboriginal history and oral tradition. When people were living together in larger and enclosed communities, history and tradition were passed on orally by the older ones, and, while the community remained together, the traditions were retained by the people. This was one of the many resistance strategies that Aboriginal people employed against the colonising forces.

This traditional period of Aboriginal resistance was overtaken by contemporary events following the 1967 Referendum which resulted in constitutional changes that established the long overdue mandate for the inclusion of Aboriginal and Torres Strait Islander people in the national census. At the same time the Referendum gave the federal government concurrent powers with the states to enact legislation dealing with Aboriginal affairs. The contemporary Aboriginal struggle for justice and equality assumed a revitalised intensity born of an increased political awareness and pride in Aboriginality.

The Queensland government's long-term plan was to gradually absorb Aboriginal people into the white community, so that Aboriginal people and their cultures would become extinct. However, this plan did not succeed, and that is another amazing part of history, namely, the extent to which Aboriginal people have been able to withstand these deliberate attempts at complete annihilation. Today, Aboriginal people still have a rich tradition of oral history, story-telling, philosophy, autobiography and biography.

Thus Aboriginal studies is now concerned with the transformation of an 'oral literature' into a written literature, without necessarily destroying the original form in the process. The written mode of expression releases material that was previously to a large extent encapsulated in a local or regional setting, and makes it available for more general distribution and reinterpretation.

Equally important in Aboriginal writing is a concern with history, with precise knowledge of the history of Aboriginal existence, gleaned if necessary from white records and prised out of white archives.

Recording the memories of elderly Aboriginals is an urgent task, otherwise much information about *Australian* history will be lost forever. It may also create a picture of what it has been like to be 'on the other side' of forced assimilationist policies, and of strategies for coping which have led to survival. Indeed, the life stories of older people can illuminate much about what it was like to live in earlier days, and how people experienced the world they knew.

During the era of Labor rule in Queensland (1915–1957), no independent Aboriginal voices were ever officially allowed to surface and make themselves heard. Not a single statement from an Aboriginal was ever reproduced in Parliament or in printed government reports or in the media during this period.[2] With the change of government in 1957 the opportunity arose to form an organisation of Aboriginals and non-Aboriginals that had the support of government, and the One People of Australia League (OPAL) was formed in 1961.

Women and members of ethnic groups and, more particularly, Aboriginal women are less likely to become famous through their work because they are under-represented as public figures, although their contribution to their own communities may have been *very great*. Rita Huggins was such a woman.

Rita Huggins was born Rita Holt on 10 August 1921 at Carnarvon Gorge via Springsure, Central Queensland. She was born of two so-called 'half-caste' parents, Albert and Rose Holt, whose traditional Bidjara-Pitjara area encompassed what is now known as the national park of Carnarvon Gorge.

Carnarvon Gorge is located approximately 600 kilometres north-west of Brisbane dissecting the sandstone tablelands of the Great Dividing Range in the Central Western Highlands of Queensland. Magic scenic attractions complement the history of Aboriginal occupancy for over 19,000 years.[3] In a tangle of nature's gorges, ranges and tablelands, a number of Aboriginal tribal groups lived. Some tribal groups living around the area were Bidjara, Kairi, Nuri, Karingbal, Kongabulla, Jiman and Wadja. Since the government removals, a comparatively small number of descendants from these tribal groups, particularly those identifying as the Bidjara, are now scattered over a wide area of Queensland and northern New South Wales.

Rita was never bestowed a tribal name that she could recall. She may well have been, but this would most certainly have become redundant when her family was forcibly removed to Barambah (as Cherbourg was known in the late 1920s). This redundancy was due to the white expectation that Aboriginal people would no longer continue their 'heathen' ways and practices, and concomitant attempts to Anglicise every aspect of their culture and lifestyle. Here too, the prime signifier of personal identification was concealed. Just as Albert and Rose were given European names, so too were Rita's brothers and sisters – Barney, Margaret, Clare, Harry, Thelma, Jimmy, Lawrence, Violet, Ruby, Oliver, Albert, Isobel and Walter.

Tindale's research into Aboriginal tribes held in the South Australian Museum has also revealed Rita as 'Rita'. Aboriginal people despair at the lack of information about their people's genealogies and tribal names like this. However, Rita was able to trace her maternal Grandmother in the Tindale documents – 'Lucy', a 'full-blood' from the Maranoa.[4]

Anguish and confusion surrounded the Holt family as they awoke one morning to the clamour of horses and troopers riding through their camp. Rita remembers her Mother shielding the children protectively from the troopers in the back of a cattle truck to Barambah.

Rita vividly recalls her aged Grandmother wailing as the 'mob' were rounded up. 'Don't take my gunduburris!* Don't take my gunduburris!' she screamed repeatedly. Much later Rita was told that her Grandmother had wandered off aimlessly into the bush that day, and was never sighted alive again. It is presumed she died alone somewhere out there of a broken heart. When her body was found it was taken to Woorabinda where her 'full-blood' relations lived. On the basis of skin colour the 'half-castes' were sent to Barambah and the 'full-bloods' to Woorabinda.[5]

This would align with the colonisers' ideology that children who

---

*   gunduburris – children

possessed strains of white blood would be easier to assimilate into European society than would their darker counterparts. Certainly, schooling was to be the prime way that Aboriginal children could be socialised and imbued with European values. The lighter-skinned children were segregated from the darker children in classes to accelerate their acceptance as white people. Teachers and missionaries were astounded when this sad strategy did not succeed.

Rita attended school from the age of eight until the age of thirteen, or Fourth Grade as it was then. Subjects taken were basic reading, writing and arithmetic, with particular emphasis on British history, Captain Cook and sewing. Happy memories of school still remain with Rita, not because of the educational content, but because it was a place where kids could socialise.

Outside of school other duties took precedence. As one of the middle ones in the family, Rita shared the household chores with her other brothers and sisters and, in that sense, the workload was fairly evenly distributed. The egalitarian nature of the family relationships was such that no one had specific jobs or ever felt 'picked on'. At a very young age Rita helped gather firewood, as well as attending to other chores which included washing up, cleaning the yard, helping prepare dinner and looking after younger brothers and sisters while her Mother rested.

Rita was sent to the mission dormitory at the relatively late age of thirteen as punishment for dating boys. Life in the dormitories was one of control, regimentation and discipline. Boys and girls were segregated and were required to do a range of domestic chores such as making their beds, rinsing soiled linen, washing and scrubbing out the dormitory and picking up papers. After breakfast the children went to school for several hours. Some playtime filled in the rest of the day before prayers, dinner and bed. The dormitory routine did its damage in its attempts to sever ties between the children and their traditional life, and the considerable time it absorbed succeeded in limiting the depth and richness of their traditional knowledge. Dormitory life also attempted to take away the disciplinary powers of the children's natural parents. Aboriginal people now were being managed, protected, taught and chastised like children and in this way lost much of the autonomy they had formerly enjoyed.

Rita did not ever feel Cherbourg was her home, as she yearned nostalgically for the days she had known in Carnarvon Gorge. A dislocated person in a sense, she was physically located at Barambah but emotionally and spiritually centred in Carnarvon Gorge. Unlike an immigrant to a new country who has chosen to relinquish her place of birth for 'greener pastures', Rita would not and could not entertain that notion. Her soul stirred for her traditional lands. She felt an outcast, a refugee in her own country, like so many other Aboriginals in the past and present and undoubtedly in the future.

Around the age of thirteen, the time came for girls to train as 'worthy housekeepers'. It was routine for girls to be placed in servitude as domestic servants by certain persons in authority. In any case, the Aboriginals' Preservation Acts 1939–1946 empowered reserve superintendents to enter employment contracts on behalf of residents, to hold funds they might have, and to control their spending. Mr Semple, the then Cherbourg superintendent, had arrangements with both local and distant policemen, pastoralists and farmers to supply a regular and steady flow of workers for those in 'need'.

Rita remembers the expectation of all the girls, whether they were of her age group or younger, that they would fulfil their roles as domestic servants. Rita's first job in 1934 entailed a long day from dawn until the late hours of the evening in the daily routine of cleaning, washing, ironing, preparing food and caring for children. Her background and the experience of her work as a domestic has, in a way, shaped the greater part of her lifestyle. Even today she does not feel comfortable and a 'whole' person unless she has spent the day in some kind of domestic activity, whether it be cooking or cleaning.

In 1940, when she was 18 years old, Rita met Jack Huggins in Brisbane. Jack was possibly the first Aboriginal person in Queensland to hold a position in the Post Office. It was not until after World War II that Rita and Jack re-met, and in 1951 they married in Ayr, north Queensland. Their union produced three children – two girls and a boy. However, Jack never fully recovered from injuries received as a prisoner-of-war, and his life with his young family was brief. He died in 1958 from a heart attack at the age of 38.

Devastated by the loss of her husband, Rita returned to Brisbane in 1959 to the comfort of her extended family network. Her family was one of the first Aboriginal families to live in Inala (now the most densely populated Aboriginal suburb in Brisbane). As the population expanded, many Aboriginal people formed their own identifiable community groups. Rita excelled at providing places where local Aboriginal families who were new to the city could get to know each other. She was able to operate in this manner under the umbrella of OPAL.

I remember all of my Mother's stories, probably much better than she realises. Not only have I heard them a hundred times over, but she is a fine story-teller, recalling every event of her life with the vividness of the present, noting each detail right down to the cut and colour of her dress. I remember her stories of being only allowed to go to Fourth Grade at school, stories of the cohesiveness of Murries on the reserve, stories of how none of them ever saw the money which was paid into their trust accounts.

I remember stories about when she met and married my Father, in the days long before he and his people were even citizens of this country; stories of the excitement of the 1967 Referendum and how Aboriginal people were politically organising themselves, stories of the love and loss of her family, and so on.

Yes, I too have lived through every one of those feelings as she related them to me.

This leads me onto my next point about how one writes about something so personal while striving for some objectivity at the same time. In Alix K. Shulman's *Was My Life Worth Living?* Emma Goldman states:

> It requires something more than personal experience to gain a philosophy or point of view from any specific event. It is the quality of our response to the event and our capacity to enter into the lives of others that help us make their lives and experiences our own.

It goes without saying that by virtue of being Rita's daughter (and a close one at that), I possess many of her experiences.

However, as Rita is a product of her time, so too am I and some of the things she may have been obliged to accept in those days, particularly the blatant patronisation, discrimination and subjugation, are like waving a red flag at a bull to me. Not that she did not have the courage to stand up for herself; the plain fact was that every obstacle was placed in her way and if she objected she would have faced the barrage of insults and humiliation thrown at Aboriginal people in those days. I'm not saying that it doesn't occur today, but the players, rules and games are different. Aboriginal people can more easily manipulate the system now. In those days you had to shut up and put up with for survival's sake.

So how do 'the oppressed' write about 'the oppressed'? I tried asking this question at an Autobiography and Biography Conference, with little success.[6] I guess it's one I have to figure out myself, but I would consider it 'the liberated' writing about 'the literated'.

In relation to my Mother's wishes, she wants to make the book as accessible to family and Aboriginal community members as possible. And in her words, 'This means no big words, little (conscious) politics and my story.' Now this is where my ego takes a bruising because, yes, it is her story, not mine. I have to constantly remind myself of that fact. How much is 'I' the writer? Then I think maybe someone else should have written Rita's life story, but neither she nor I could ever have conceded that one. I believe she has had enough tampering in her life by whites and needs no further investigation or intrusion.

In deliberations about the title I had thought of various titles such as *A Misfortunate Life*, *Dr Jekyll and Mrs Hyde* and *The Sequel to Mommie Dearest*, among others. Seriously, the title of her book will be *Auntie Rita*, the term she is affectionately known by. It is a sign not only of extended family and community relations but is a title given in the greatest respect to Elders of our social world.

My search has been for what I can give my Mother in return for her love, strength, wisdom and inspiration to me. I have found the answer in writing her biography. Her contribution to her people and to Australia has been immense. She may not have been the public figure that someone like Charles Perkins is, but she has been a public figure to family and Aboriginal community groups, and to her this is where it counts. She has certainly been the inspiration of my life.

Her life history is important, indeed *precious*, and the act of recording and publishing it is in Aboriginal English 'pretty deadly Tidda business' – which translated means wonderful, strong Black woman stuff.

But You Couldn't Possibly ...

When I was young I had dreams of being something that was potentially of goodness and of course helpful to my people. The ballerina and newspaper boy didn't turn out so I had to dream of other things. One most important factor was to gain an education in order to get what I wanted. However, the straight-through road is not possible for most Aboriginal children. Teachers in my time had low expectations of how much Indigenous children could achieve through the Western education system. I was a victim of this. What gave me more determination was the people who said we couldn't do it or you couldn't possibly ... (This was written in 1992.)

—

In November 1958 Jack Huggins died of a massive heart attack in Ayr, north Queensland. Jack had been a prisoner-of-war in Burma/Thailand, one of the many Aboriginal men who had fought and died for their country while back home their children were being denied access to a full education, atrocities were occurring daily against Aboriginal people, and Aboriginal people were not even citizens of their own country. At age 38 Jack died and was not afforded the status of an Australian citizen.

In the 1940s Jack was employed in the Post Office. It was a rare sight to see a Black man in any public office in those days. Rita and

Jack's union produced three children. I was the middle one. Rita also had two daughters by a previous relationship.

I grew up in a single-parent household which possessed a very strong mother. She instilled into us the importance of pride in Aboriginality; to fight to overcome racism and other injustices; to be proud of who we were and never duck into a corner and hide it; to deal with white people as if we were equal to them, and to involve all children in Aboriginal activities from a young age.

My early childhood was 'ordinary' in an Aboriginal sense but 'different' Anglo-wise. Different because we were not 'Anglo-Australian'. Ordinary because many Aboriginal families are single-parent families and we are all one big family.

Rita returned to Brisbane in 1959, after Jack's death, to the comfort of her extended family network. The extended family provided solace for her grief and an anchor for her children. Without this, Jack's loss would have been more unbearable to her. Rita thus became a 'war widow' and received a pension all her life.

My Father's death influenced my life more than I ever realised. He died from war injuries inflicted in a needless war, and before he could witness some of the more positive steps taken to address the injustices to Aboriginal people: the 1967 Federal Referendum, recognising (for the first time in Anglo-Australian history) Aboriginal people as citizens, the Northern Territory Land Rights cases and many other historical events.

Throughout my life my driving force has always been my Aboriginality in whatever I do. I am nurtured and guided by it. My foremost identity is as an Aboriginal. My family gave me a strong and proud upbringing and a belief that to be Aboriginal was the greatest honour in the world. We just had to educate other people into believing this was true.

I've wanted to be many things. Perhaps being too many things to too many people has impeded my progress: when offers come up I see them as equally important and find it hard to say no.

While all my immediate family have a keen sense of pride in their Aboriginality, I am the most public and outspoken member. I've sought out, and followed through, any opportunities I could. My political activism has been my identity; commitment to my people and community my entire existence.

I knew I'd be working in some field of Aboriginal affairs, as I could not be a whole person if I didn't. (As a child I had fantasies of being an air-hostess, a paper boy – and a ballerina of all things – and I thank God those ideas never came to fruition.)

Two strong Black women have been my role models: my Mother, instilling me with the fight and determination to succeed, and my cousin Lillian Holt. Lillian, eleven years older than me, was a fighter in Aboriginal affairs long before it was fashionable. As a young girl I admired her immensely, her wisdom, strength, tenacity, good humour and unconditional willingness to share all her hopes, fears and aspirations about the plight of our people. With much pride I say that I didn't need to look outside my family to find role models.

From the time I was born I have been political. Aboriginal people are born political. Political awareness and action is a way of life. I could not hide, nor did I ever want to hide, the fact that I was Aboriginal, and I always knew who and what I am. Perhaps the greatest influence in my life has come from many bigoted people who have low expectations of my race. It's the rising above that I find the greatest liberating force.

In Year 10 at high school I saw the senior mistress to discuss future schooling and other vocational options. I told her I'd like to complete Year 12. She laughed: 'Oh but you couldn't possibly do that!' My grades were good and I was taken aback. Bewildered, I asked why not. 'Because you're Aboriginal and Aboriginals have got no brains.' I felt dehumanised and powerless. At 15 years old I had neither the words nor the guts to challenge her. What a different story it would be today. I crawled out of the office, my dreams shattered. She erected a stumbling block in my psyche which remained through Year 11: I thought I was too dumb to achieve any scholastic accomplishments.

Determined to go on and seek further challenges in life, at twenty-six I enrolled at The University of Queensland. I began to receive high distinctions. I realised I was not dumb or biologically mentally inferior to non-Aboriginals, and grew to love my studies and the challenge of university. I graduated with a BA (Hons) in History and Women's Studies, and went on to complete a Diploma of Education. So many Aboriginal people have been discouraged because others cannot see their goals as achievable and equal to others. My story is not an isolated case. It's happened and continues to happen through people's notions of vast superiority over Blacks. It is this concern that largely motivates my work: to prove that we are just as good and even better than most.

At school I felt different because other kids never saw or liaised with their relations very often; they didn't stay in crowded houses; they didn't know what it was like to wear the same dress to school every day and what it was like to go without food. The older I got the more 'different' I felt from other people. It was a growing political awareness to feel I was different. It was also a strength and a comfort to know I wasn't the same as everyone else. Some differences are creative and should be respected for what they are. The colour of my skin and my Aboriginal features are integral components of my identity. There are beautiful aspects of my culture like sharing, non-competitiveness, non-materialism and respect for others as human beings which I never saw reciprocated in Anglo society. I never wanted to be white because my dignity and spirit would be dead.

Brisbane became home. The extended family left the Cherbourg Aboriginal Reserve (which was in the heart, or should I say thorn, of the old Bjelke-Petersen electorate of Barambah) for the greater freedoms of city life and employment.

Aboriginal people in Brisbane faced difficulties, being 'newcomers' and being primarily rural or small-town and reserve people moving into an urban area. In addition, Aboriginal people also faced racial prejudice and discrimination. My family moved house fourteen times in three years, due largely to discrimination by landlords and their intolerance of the sharing of homes with transient relatives and friends.

Every few years I like to go 'walkabout' to recharge my batteries, to a place where I am not well known within the Aboriginal community and where I can find some space to do what is personally fulfilling, like studying, writing and working. This is necessary because, among other stresses, many community expectations are placed upon Aboriginal people who are successful and educated in the Western sense. They are in demand to render assistance, such as writing submissions, organising conferences, lecturing to recruits, sitting on committees, and talking to groups most often in their local communities.

I survive by breaking away to another city. When I enter another state the pressure is immediately lifted. There's more autonomy, fewer ties to my mob. Nonetheless, I can't be away too long. Brisbane is my home and the centre to which I gravitate. Also, my family is here, and I miss my community and other Queensland Murries if I am away too long.

In 1978 and 1979 I worked for the National Aboriginal Council (NAC) secretariat in Canberra. In 1984 it was Canberra again, in the Department of Aboriginal Affairs (DAA), and in 1988 and 1989 I studied at Flinders University in Adelaide. The moves have been well timed. In 1988 I had to escape from Queensland during the Bicentennial because I couldn't stand the hype and hypocrisy associated with the celebrations. Being somewhere else

I could become a recluse. I tried hard to ignore it and concentrate on the 60,000-plus years of Dreaming rather than the 200 years of nightmares following colonisation.

A magical highlight of my life was participating in the Aboriginal march in Sydney, January 1988. An overwhelming sense of pride engulfed me that day. I woke up with bursting emotions, as if I were standing on the shore the day Phillip and the 'First Fleet' arrived, or even when Captain Cook set foot. I said to one of the four Aboriginal Sisters who had travelled down with me from Brisbane, 'Do you feel how I do?' With tears in her eyes she said, 'Exactly.' We needed no more words to know how we felt the same emotion.

We marched that day for our ancestors and for the generations to come. When we turned the corner into Belmore Park, we saw a huge sea of non-Aboriginal faces, waiting and ready to march with us. We marched proudly in solidarity in the colours of black, yellow and red, never before realising the number of our supporters. The media reports stated that only 20,000 marched but it was more like 60,000. Aboriginal people came in droves, the best way they could manage, from thousands of miles around Australia. The solidarity that Invasion Day turned my mourning into joy and gave me great hope for the future and our children.

Establishing the new office of Indigenous Women in the old Department of Aboriginal Affairs – now ATSIC (the Aboriginal and Torres Strait Islanders Commission) – has been one of my greatest achievements. I headed a national unit comprising fifty Commonwealth Employment Program (CEP) Aboriginal and Islander women to assess the needs of women, youth and children throughout Australia. A 100-page report specified the needs and concerns of Aboriginal and Islander women in Australia. Permanent positions were then created in DAA regional, area and head offices.

At DAA my duties were to direct the Aboriginal Women's Unit, to formulate and develop aims and policies in respect of the social development of Aboriginal women and children; to assist in ensuring that the department's functional programs reflected the needs and concerns of Aboriginal women and children; to co-ordinate the implementation and development of appropriate programs and strategies; to undertake appropriate investigations and analyses of policy issues. During 1984 I travelled extensively throughout Australia attending Aboriginal women's groups and advising them in setting up their own organisations. Highly visible and growing numbers of Aboriginal and Islander women's organisations now exist within community and bureaucratic structures, serving the aspirations of our women and children.

The white men in DAA put obstacles in our way. It was a fight every day to educate them that Aboriginal women had vital statements to make about health, housing, education, employment and areas which required attention. Of the fifty women employed, about five had tertiary experience, ten had been employed before, and the rest were previously on pensions or benefits or involved in home-duties and had limited education. With a crew like this the white staff thought it was doomed to fail. It didn't. It's still there – thriving.

Simultaneously with our project, the Office of the Status of Women employed other Aboriginal women to perform a similar task. I had suspected that this duplication was designed to create havoc, fighting and non-productivity between the two bodies. However, the competition served only to extract the best possible information from women in the field. The thoroughness of this information was published in *Women's Business*. Overseeing the Aboriginal Women's Task Force was an all-Aboriginal Women's Steering Committee of which I was a member. The hard slog and the solidarity of all women who worked with me in the Aboriginal Women's Unit will always be remembered. The innovative nature of our job meant we had to be the pioneers. We began with nothing. It was a milestone for Black women.

I see myself as a multi-faceted and multi-talented person and an advocate for Aboriginal people. Other people see me as a role model for Aboriginals, particularly young Black women who have aspirations of working in community affairs. They see that I have done much along the way: establishing community-based organisations, organising the first International Indigenous Women's Conference, completing tertiary studies, achieving a high position in the public service, writing articles in journals and chapters in history books, and being a member of national and state Aboriginal advisory boards.

Out of all this, the most important aspect of my life is other Aboriginal people and their existence in this country. My greatest achievement came at a time when I knew we could accomplish great things. I was relatively young – 27 years of age, and full of energy – when I worked in Canberra as the national co-ordinator of the AWU. A precedent was established where a government department was prepared to look at the specific needs of Aboriginal and Torres Strait women, then turn them into policy.

My life now is a natural progression of my experiences in childhood and growing up. It's a new direction that Aboriginal women are taking and directing: challenging white feminists about what the women's movement's exclusion of us has meant, issues of race, propriety of knowledge and information. It also means looking at ways in which we can form alliances with each other.

In my political activism I have not felt different from other Aboriginal people. But when engaging in debates about feminism I feel very different from Aboriginal people. The isolation of being usually the only Aboriginal woman at feminist and women's studies conferences is unbearable at times because I prefer the solidarity and group nature of Aboriginal society and sisterhood. I wish there were 'more troops in the hills' and reinforcements lining up but the signs are not encouraging.

I would like to see the Aboriginal history of our country taken seriously, placing Aboriginal people as significant and restoring their past to a respectful place. I would like to rid the world of racism and capitalism to make it a better place for us all. This means 'changing the world'. Changing Australia would be a good starting point.

My activism is not restricted. On the contrary, it is becoming far broader. While many activities and actions I have undertaken have not been deliberate, I sense components are being channelled in particular directions. One concerns Aboriginal women's representations within the women's movement (that is, the exploration of race within the movement), another my writing of Aboriginal women's history.

Given the opportunity, I would have studied at tertiary level much earlier in life, say five years earlier. Then I would be five years advanced and ready for my next step. But I am laying the foundations for greater things to come. As for my community activities, I'll stay in them until I die, because they are my bloodline.

Life is a game of chance and I have been in the right place at the right time, and have given it one hundred per cent. Being thorough is what's important, and following through no matter how small something may appear because it could be a matter of life and death for others. We must fight against all oppressions, but we usually focus on those we know and feel the most: mine is racism against Aboriginal people.

Are All the Women White?

My two role models in writing have been the African American writers Audre Lorde and bell hooks. So imagine how I felt when my friend Nicola Joseph from the then Coming Out Show *on ABC Radio rang me in 1996 to ask if I would like to talk to bell hooks about Black feminism in Australia and the United States. Like the singer Phoebe Snow, whose dulcet tones motivated me during the typing up of the manuscript of* Auntie Rita, *bell hooks was legendary and inspirational to me. Her powerful writing of compassion and perception and her sheer dedication and belief in the value of her work both in academia and the community were goals I strove for.*

—

Nicola: In tonight's program African American feminist bell hooks talks with Aboriginal activist and writer Jackie Huggins. Welcome to the *Coming Out Show*, I'm Nicola Joseph.

bell hooks is one of America's leading Black women writers. She wrote her first book at the age of nineteen after being frustrated at the lack of Black feminist writing available in the United States. She has written several books in the twenty years which followed. bell spent her childhood in the deep south of America, a region notorious for its racism, even today. Her feminism is revolutionary to say the least and it's inspired more by her life experience than by theory read in books.

Jackie Huggins is an Aboriginal woman from Queensland, another region notorious for its racist history. She is a writer, an historian and a woman who is struggling to find a platform to speak from which is both non-racist and non-sexist. This is a difficult place to find in Australia even today. The mainstream women's movement has done little to dismantle its racism so it's not surprising that Aboriginal and migrant women often don't call themselves feminists.

Jackie: I was recently asked at a conference why is it that Aboriginal women don't participate in the more theoretical debates that go on between Black and white women in this country. My initial response to that was that white women are colonists too, they are part of the dominant culture which continually oppresses us in this country and that the theoretical issues and writings seem far too abstract at this stage to form some kind of bridge that we can get together to cross to overcome and start talking as women.

I think in Australia at the moment the race issue is very paramount. It's a very exciting time. There are clusters of feminists out there who are willing to acknowledge that and willing to give us some part of their resources, to start sharing their resources with us. However, this has created a great rejection in some areas by Black women because we have been excluded for so long that we don't want to be party to that any more. They see it as an impossible situation that we actually can work with women of other colours, women of difference, and while I think it's very important that we break down the white dominant structures that exist in this country, it's a two-way thing and we're willing – certainly I am – to negotiate and to share stuff about women, about feminism and we're just starting to scratch the surface. Feminists in this country are now starting to show their colours, I believe, in terms of who is going to acknowledge our oppression as Aboriginal women, doubly oppressed with racism and sexism.

bell: Let me give you an example of what happens here. In Women's Studies programs, for example, at universities people will acknowledge race until you suggest, 'Wait a minute, only white women are in positions of power in this.' What happens is people will want to hire a Black woman to be the secretary or to be the lowest person on the faculty level. And we'll say to them but wait a minute, aren't you conscious of the fact that what you're doing here is saying we'll include you as long as you maintain a subordinate position in relation to us? That's the kind of institutional manifestation of racism within the women's movement that I think is very difficult for us to change because it's finally about power and people willing to give up power as opposed to just paying lip service to the idea of race.

Jackie: I think it's very important that we look at the way in which women are prepared to give up power. If there are any antidotes for how we do that, bell, I'm very interested in hearing about it.

bell: Well, one of the things I feel we have to really point to is we have to look at examples of white women who do give up power, because unless people have some kind of notion that it can be done, that one can survive – I think that people have a great fear that if they give up power they'll be diminished in some way. A lot of the new work I've been doing is trying to take examples from women I've worked with – like one of the things I did is one of my white woman colleagues that I worked with here at the college where I teach, we felt that we had come together and been able to work well together because we shared a common class background, both of us coming from poor working class experiences. So we decided that we would do a conversation together, Jackie, much like the conversation we are doing now, only we decided to sit and talk and then type it up so that people could understand that it is possible for a Black woman and a white woman to come together, work together, have issues that we disagree on but still find points of solidarity. One of the reasons we did this was that we felt that it's not enough for us either as Black women or for white women to critique the situation, but we also have to take some concrete steps in the direction of coalition and solidarity and understand how those steps are made.

One of the things we talked about was what breaks down the relationship between coloniser and colonised. We felt like trust was very important and that the trust really between a Black woman and a white woman, a lot of it has to come from white women indicating where they stand on the question of race. And that means I don't want a white woman to want to be my friend when she hasn't yet thought about unlearning her racism. I want her to think about unlearning her racism and then approach me. Otherwise, then I feel like I'm being put once again in, you know, 'I want you to be my friend so I can have someone who will help me unlearn my racism'. Once again, this puts Black women in the kind of maid service position, as 'help me to do something that will benefit me' rather than the kind of approach of mutuality that would say we can be bonded together because we are both committed to the anti-racist struggle and the anti-sexist struggle and that those two things, those two commitments, converge and undergird and strengthen one another.

Nicola: How do you feel about that, Jackie? I mean, you're constantly put in that position of being the person that's got to teach people how to undo their racism.

Jackie: Quite frankly I'm drained by it. I'm really intolerant of being the object all the time. I'm usually the only token Black woman who goes to these kinds of feminist conferences or Women's Studies conferences and they turn on me as if to say, well you're the only Black in the room, therefore you're the expert – you should know all the answers to the questions that we're going to fire on you and they actually do that. They seize upon me and ask me all these questions, saying what can I do, continually asking how I can solve their problems, and it's quite draining to tell you the truth. I feel really exhausted by it. Like there's a magical prescription for doing so.

I say to white women now, 'It's not for me to educate you into doing something about the problem. If you admit that, yes, you are white supremist or racist then it is your obligation to go out and do things yourself.' I think people come up with a lot of expectations that I'm supposed to wave the magic wand and prepare these magical formulas that will teach white women how to be non-racist and how to accept us as women. And that's why a lot of Aboriginal women don't participate fully or don't have anything to do with the white women's movement here in Australia, because they see it as assimilationist and they haven't yet given us the respect and dignity that we deserve as women in this country.

Yes, so it's a problem of getting away from being an object and now being the subject and I was hoping that bell might be able to provide some comments on that.

bell: Well, one of the first comments I would like to make is that what's so wonderful about this introduction to being among and with and talking to Australian women for me is that I'm talking to another Black woman, because I think that for us as Black women, becoming subject first means that we recognise ourselves, not that we position ourselves as the little helpmate to white women who want to understand racism but that we understand our own positioning as the victims of racism and colonisation and that we are constantly engaged in a process of decolonisation.

That means that we first and foremost have to look to one another to affirm ourselves as subject and I think once we do that, as we're doing in this conversation, there's much more space for us to think about what we can then share of ourselves with those white women who are trying to unlearn racism, and I would say unlearn sexism too because a lot of these attitudes of seeing the Black woman as a servant combines racism and sexism.

So I think I feel, Jackie, probably like you that I'm willing to help anybody who is trying to decolonise themselves or anyone who is a coloniser who is trying to work against that. If I see that they are doing, you know, ninety per cent or they're willing to do a lot of work themselves rather than turning to me for a shortcut – and I think this has been a major problem here, with white women wanting to take shortcuts and not wanting to do the actual work of saying 'How do I climb this mountain?', not to ask you what it's like at the top of the mountain.

Jackie: Yes. And I think that white women shouldn't expect anything from Black women that doesn't give us some kind of empowerment as well. I say these days to offers of speaking, offers of going along to things, then yes as a Black woman, what am 'I' getting out of this. Am I getting something too which will empower me as a Black woman? Those are the conditions on which I operate these days.

bell: Recently I gave a talk where a white woman was saying to me she was very upset by the notion that somehow Black people did not want to affirm her for being anti-racist and I was saying that as long as you still feel that you have to be rewarded by us in some way for your anti-racist commitment, you're acting like it's something you're doing for us, which is very different from doing for yourself. I said to her that as a Black woman who has been totally committed to spreading the message of feminism to Black women, I don't feel that Black women owe it to me to affirm this, because in fact this is my political commitment. It is deeply what I believe.

While I want to share feminist thinking with Black women, I'm not devastated when Black women who don't know about feminism and challenge me, don't immediately clap their hands and tell me how wonderful I am, because the point is that's not why I'm a feminist and it can't be why any white woman is anti-racist – that she wants to be affirmed and loved by Black women.

I think that's very important for us to think about, particularly in the US where I think political commitment is often not a part of how we think about culture or how we think about being liked or being embraced and affirmed in these very personal ways and not in ways that say perhaps it's important to take a stand on a cause. Be oppositional, even if no one else affirms you.

You know, I sat at a dinner table with ten Black women the other day who were all saying to me, 'You know we think you're crazy to be thinking about feminism' because they see it as such a white woman thing. But it's not like I felt like I'm going to drop talking to Black women about sexism because they weren't approving of me or liking me or making me feel good, because that's not what political commitment is about.

Jackie: With Aboriginal women here, you go to them and they'll say, 'I'm not really a feminist', but what they're saying is they really are but we have terms in which we describe ourselves as Aboriginal women and those terms are Aboriginal words like *Tiddas, miminy, kudgeri* and *montajula*. Now all those words mean 'very strong Aboriginal woman'. Women tend to shy away very much from the word feminist because we see it as a white feminist interpretation and a white word. If we can get the language in which to say Aboriginal women are feminist, that they are actually living it, they are talking it,

71

they are breathing it every day of their lives, then I think that's going to be quite acceptable to them.

Also, you know, there is the other side of the coin where you have, if we're going to be understood by the dominant structure, the dominant powers that be … I think if we can get a language going together as Black women in this country, I think it's going to be pretty deadly, which means pretty magical.

—

Jackie: Our men, and dare we get on to that subject, our men are starting to get a bit agitated with seeing Black women in this country gravitating towards feminism rather than back to the Black environment, the Black community if you will. The whole problem of where one is disloyal to their people or appears to be disloyal to their people is something that I, certainly as a Black woman, have had to grapple with. Probably not nearly as long and as varied as bell has.

I'd like to ask you, bell, in being reflective about what you're doing as a Black feminist, has it been an issue with you, that you at times had to choose? I don't believe we should be making choices about where we're lying.

bell: First I would like to say to you, Jackie, that I think the strongest aspect of who I am – in terms of the very rural Black community that I come from, that keeps me sort of grounded – is that I really love my community and I love Black people. And I found that wherever I go people don't just shut me out, because they see that feeling of love and concern. It's measured by a concern for the fate of Black people globally as well as a concern for the plight and fate of Black people in the US. In some of my writings I have been talking about love as a force, not as a sentimental romantic feeling but as a political force that can mediate some of the tensions that arise.

I might go into a Black city and begin talking about gender and feel the tensions. People start getting kind of hostile, but when I frame my concerns in a way that reflect a concern for the welfare of Black people, there is much more openness to those concerns. I'm like a lot of people. I don't want us to give up the term 'feminism', because I think that Black women have a tremendous vision to offer the world in terms of how we might revolutionise gender, race, etc. If we abandon the larger terminology for a specific terminology that only we can use as a kind of inside group, then I think we risk further marginalisation – not from something we might call white feminism but from a global movement of feminism which is about ending sexism, and we might need to be the movers and the shakers shaping how that global movement might be. This means that we don't just have a vision to offer around Blackness. We have an overall vision to offer.

We have a lot to say about feeding the planet, about questions of housing, all of those things that are issues that may have a specific dimension. I mean, if I wanted to talk about housing for Black people in the United States, I would frame my discussion very differently than if I was going to talk about the problems of the homeless in general. But what I feel is that I have a vision to offer about both those things and I don't want anyone to deny me my right to that multiple vision.

It's very important for us to insist on, otherwise we risk always being marginalised, and as we remain marginalised, we remain subject to certain forms of domination and victimisation …

Nicola: Maybe I'm a bit more pessimistic than you. I look at where a lot of whites from the Civil Rights Movement in America are now, and indeed some of the white South Africans who fought ten years ago, where they are now.

bell: I don't think as Black people we can afford the luxury of that kind of cynicism, because I find that when privileged people are cynical, they can go about their lives and be cynical, but I think what happens when oppressed people are cynical is that nihilism becomes a kind of genocidal force in our lives. There's a certain kind of despair that Black people feel in the United States right now and poor people, underclass Black people, feel it the most.

From my standpoint, I have to see the production of an ideology of hope as also part of what it means to be a political person right now, because unless people feel that there is a possibility of change and transformation, then there's nothing to lift yourself up for. You know, there's nothing to struggle for. So you have this massive drug addiction that we're having in a lot of poor Black communities – because what's the point, why shouldn't you kill yourself with drugs or why shouldn't you kill yourself in meaningless wars, mini wars over Nike tennis shoes, if there's no reason to hope, you know, if we can't have a redemptive vision. That's what I call it.

Martin Luther King offered to Black people and to white people and other groups of people in this culture a redemptive vision, which I think says that perhaps a vision might be an impossible one to fully achieve but working for it is what makes concrete transformation real.

Jackie: Yes, I think as bell said, if we give up the fight then what are we fighting for? As Black people we're born into a situation where we have to be continual fighters, continual battlers for the rest of our days. We're born as political people and I think that, yes, white people can become complacent with the fact that they're doing a fairly good job in terms of dealing with their own racism and dealing with the situations of Blacks in this country, whereas for Aboriginal people it's a continual tussle. I wake up every day feeling defensive about what the hell's going to go on now, today.

Nicola: Are you positive at all?

Jackie: Yes. Yes I have to be and I have to continue to love what I'm doing and that is writing and that is struggling to get our voices heard, to not continue to be silenced like we have been in the past. And now I think the Bicentennial has opened up so many questions about the acknowledgement that there are actually Blackfellas living in this country and that we do have rights and that we want to be heard now. I think if we don't continue to fight, then our struggle is lost.

bell: When I first learned about Australian Aborigines as a girl, I learned about them from Mills & Boon romances. It says a lot about how much we've changed that I can actually be talking to Jackie as two women of consciousness, two Black revolutionary women. But I think we have to also look at how far we've come even as we acknowledge how far we have to go, because that's where the hope lies. For me it's exciting. This moment tonight is exciting because it's a moment of solidarity. It's a moment I've always dreamed about, as I've made it a point to learn about Australian Aborigines precisely because of feeling the diasporic connections between us as Black people on the planet.

Yet that learning had to go beyond simply looking at white representations of Australian Aborigines. I think that it's a kind of magical moment. I've been telling everybody that I was going to have this conversation with Jackie because it meant so much to me as a sign of Black self-determination, of a move that we're making on our own behalf and in solidarity with someone like you who helped make this moment possible.

I think it's perhaps difficult for white women to understand the degree of isolation that comes to Black women who begin to advocate a revolutionary feminism. Because here we are walking this tightrope where on the one hand we know that white feminism has a component that is supportive of imperialism and racism and colonisation. On the other hand, we know that in many Black communities globally there is a crippling male domination that is hurting to women and children, and that when we start trying to press against that and oppose it, we don't want to reinforce racist stereotypes about Black men. We don't want to make it seem that Black men are somehow more sexist than other men in the world. It's a very difficult position to inhabit both theoretically and practically in daily life. Not only is it extreme isolation sometimes but I think we also live with extreme stress and it's a very hard thing to know when we need to take off time for ourselves.

Jackie, I really heard you when you said you were tired, because again and again I hear Black women say that who are trying to advance both the anti-racist struggle and the anti-sexist struggle. At times we just feel deeply weary and it's moments like these when we can come together and let it be known and sort of testify that in fact we are not alone. We can feel our spirits renewed and that's also very important to the struggle, that moment of renewal when you pause and recognise that you're not alone.

Jackie: Yes bell, we understand how we can talk about feminism and sexism together as Black women. We have certain apparatuses like now when we are talking through radio. There are people we don't wish sometimes to allow into our space, who are not going to actually run with what we are saying and believe that that's us speaking through how we're feeling as Black women who are simultaneously being oppressed through racism and sexism. I don't feel quite comfortable talking to a general audience, and I guess that's part of my growth, about the issues that override us in relation to sexism from Black men, because of the very fact that it creates all these kinds of racist stereotypes.

But as Black women we can get together and have a good old – you probably don't know this term – a good old barney, about how we're feeling comfortable with that.

I'd just like to say one more thing to sum up what I've been attempting to say to you, and that is I think as all women we have the opportunity to forge the only struggle that is of importance to everybody – the struggle against oppression per se. If women all embrace that goal, we will win. Feminism that has the elimination of oppression as its agenda, rather than just one or more of its symptoms, truly transcends any other critical ideology. I only hope for the future and that's why I'm continuing to do the work that I do, knowing that Black women have that to offer, and if given the respect, the dignity, the resources and the commitment from other feminists, whether they be Anglos or migrant feminists, then it will surely come.

Nicola: You've been listening to bell hooks and Jackie Huggins. bell's books are published by Southend Press. Her most recent book released in Australia is called *Yearning.* Keep an eye out for Jackie Huggins' book which she has been writing with her Mother, Aunty Rita Huggins. It's due for release later in the year.

Reflections of Lilith

Written in an Aboriginal framework, trying for the humour

Over the years I have attended numerous conferences where the mandatory requirement has been a conference paper. A paper called 'Defying the Ethnographic Ventriloquists' was delivered by Kay Saunders and myself at Melbourne University at the Lilith Conference. Instant relief came after presenting it and this time I was caught up with some feelings still unresolved which I had to let go of. After an almost sleepless night I attempted to get rid of the gripping sensation that was overtaking me. 'Reflections', written in 1993, was just that, a long hard look at life and the emotions of being an Indigenous person.

—

It was one of those fine, rainy, windy, fine, windy, trinary oppositional days in Melbourne. I had been attending the Lilith Conference, where a joint paper was given with my good friend and (wo)mentor Kay Saunders, called 'Defying the Ethnographic Ventriloquists: Race, Gender and the Legacies of Ventriloquism'. Yes, it was one of those heavy topics and titles used to perplex, stimulate and motivate cultural cognitive frameworks.

I usually take long walks for purely therapeutic purposes – to clear the head and ease the loneliness of being away from my family for more than one week. This Sunday morning I took a safe stroll from my college residence to Brunswick to find a cappuccino and satisfy another equally delectable craving – for a Brisbane *Courier-Mail*. Safe is the operative word here as it was straight up the road, and easy to find, even though I have the most useless sense of direction one could hope to be born with – not like in the old days when we never used maps. What a tourist I've become in my own land.

Suffering from 'new city' alienation syndrome I wandered into a sparsely furnished coffee shop where I was confronted by a table of old men who were speaking loudly in their mother tongue which obviously wasn't English. They were sitting at the back of the cafe laughing and talking with 'ethnic' music playing in the background. Since they appeared to be absolutely enjoying each other's company, I figured that this must be their little secret weekend hideaway spurning the outside world.

I continued to feel dislocated and disoriented, not knowing where I was or whose neighbourhood I was in, since I never even saw a single Koori to ask, 'Hey cus, where the hell am I?' In all honesty, not having been exposed to multiculturalism in any real way in Brisbane, I tended to take on board the Anglo attitude to this scenario: 'They all look the same to me anyhow'.

The gentleman serving greeted me: 'Good morning – well we don't know really now, do we?', as he peered through the misty window. I was becoming more accustomed to the fact that Melburnians, while circumspect, are especially proud of their lousy weather. It certainly was the topic of the day if people knew I came from Queensland – 'Sunny one day, but racist all the others.'

By this time I had changed my order to a cafe latte rather than an ironically stereotyping cappuccino, and my thoughts reverted to the old men. Uncharacteristically, I was overcome by emotion as the thoughts of colonisation invaded my solitude and spoilt my pleasure at feeling comfortable in a place which wasn't necessarily Aboriginal nor Anglo. I thought of what it was like not to have a language, and what those bastards (whites) have done and continue to do to us in this country we all call home. This infliction of emotion allowed me to think how lucky some immigrants were to have retained their languages despite the colonisers' insistence that they discard them and their cultures, that they be Australian, and speak Australian or proper English.

'Up you white fellas (excuse me, I mean Anglos)!' I thought. (If I learned anything at the conference it was not to be so loose when using the term 'white'). 'You sucked the life and land out of us, but hopefully colonisation this time round won't be so easy.' Suddenly this rush of emotion produced an uncontrollable stream of tears which conflicted with the controlled public image of self which had prevailed at the conference proceedings the day before.

As I wiped my wet cheeks with a symbolic red serviette, in Kay's terms 'the male voice of Nationality' spoke to me. Hang on, why was I feeling like this? What was going through my head? The more I went on the more confused I got! I was senseless because rationality was totally lost – I wasn't pressured to conform, and therefore I abandoned all reasoning.

It was time to pay up and as I did I noticed a poster of an Italian soccer team behind the counter. It excused me from the rudeness, stemming from my ignorance, of inquiring as to the proprietor's bloodline or his place of origin. My dilemma was over and the old man's ethnic origin was reinforced by the 11 o'clock Italian mass sign at the church across the road.

As I wandered back from the piazza (deadly or what?) the sun was now shining and the wind had dropped to a soothing breeze. Needless to say I never did find my *Courier-Mail* that day, but I got a huge dose of ethnicity. I thought in retrospect how influenced I was by the Lilith conference, where non-Anglo women dominated the contribution and participation. There was a 200 per cent increase in

Aboriginal women's participation – the number has risen to a grand total of three. The speakers comprised six ethnic minority women, two WASPs and three Aboriginal women ('and a partridge in a pear tree'), which was the first time we'd ever dominated the colonisers.

A great strain had been lifted off me as I didn't feel in as much of a minority or as isolated as I previously have when addressing feminist conferences. The challenging and dynamic paper that my two Koori Tiddas presented was a gift, of which I was justifiably proud. Someone said how courageous they were to speak, and I reckon the same applied to the WASPs, sitting back and quietly squirming in their chairs – not all, not all, I won't homogenise WASPs here. Besides, all the WASPs I know personally were the converted, but we can never presume that for an instant of the entire audience. What's that white handbags? So for all that has been achieved by the women's movement in Australia, it has meant precious little to non-Anglo women. We still remain locked into the 'them' and 'us' stranglehold, and nothing can progress until there is a shift in this ghetto we call invisibilising race.

While the adrenalin and the raw emotion and nervous energy were still surging, I penned this paper after returning to my room. I recalled how slack my post-conference comments, recorded by the ABC's *Coming Out Show*, were. (Sorry Anna. If only you'd asked me now when I'm fresh and while that reggae song 'I Can See Clearly Now' is reverberating in my mind allowing me to crystallise the dimensions of my soul, *yuki* – [look out].)

That afternoon I treated myself to a good comedy, *Sister Act*, starring the superb Whoopi Goldberg, who I met in Adelaide after she demanded to meet with some Aboriginal women because she had seen the trinkets we had made in the shops, so where were we, and what did whites have to hide? This was around the time that I had spoken not once but twice to bell hooks (name dropper), who called ME a Black woman revolutionary like her on a Radio

National telephone interview organised by the ABC's Nicola Joseph.

At 2 am on Monday morning I was awoken by an urge to go to the toilet, followed by another natural bodily function which personally afflicts me – that of expression through writing. I still pondered on the conference but rather than the positive aspects I was recalling it in negative terms and something was amiss. As usual, at the pre-dinner drinks and conference dinner I found myself surrounded by dislocated 'others' who had by then become the dominant forces. I was also revelling in the fact that I didn't feel drained or tired after the event; rather it was Kay who slept for two days after (*gamon* – just joking). We dissected and post-mortemed the day's events. The main criticism was that some of the theoretical discourse had been constructed in a totally alien way which only served the purpose of those 'in the know' of academia – although even the majority of academics (under duress) later confessed that they couldn't understand it either. I realise it takes years of hard work to accomplish such an understanding and I truly admire those who are able to do it. The deconstruction of language is a complex sub-culture for academics of any race, gender, class or sexuality.

However, most of us (and the honest ones) were still feeling like we'd been shot by a tranquilliser gun. My eyes searched the room for an affirming non-verbal sign that someone else wasn't understanding it either. When I think about it, it was very polite that day. I looked first at my Koori Tiddas who were smiling at each other. I looked for my Anglo pals who sat fidgeting. After what seemed like an eternity and by the grace of God, there she was – a woman who shall remain nameless – I will always remember her as that bold woman who swung back on her chair and gave me that knowing signal, that sign I had been thirsting for. I felt normal, restored and whole again.

My academic training has been in history, anthropology and

women's studies, but my holistic training and combat grounding has been in the Aboriginal community. Unfortunately and fortunately, my structural and strategic positions have changed somewhat, and while I am still in the firing line I do not enter into every dogfight which goes on in my community. It was an academic conference, but as a public intellectual myself, I endeavour to make language accessible to everybody who cares to listen, especially if Aboriginal people are in the audience – for they are my greatest mandates, benchmarks and critics.

Perhaps one of the reasons why I have resisted a career in academia is that I find the esoteric world of living, speaking, thinking, writing and acting-out most uncomfortable and problematic. I realise also that as minorities we have to challenge the dominant power structures – which are white/Anglo, male and female – that oppress us, and turn their structures and languages against them. But I would hope that as minority women we can utilise communication styles which do not intimidate, alienate and silence our own.

Personally, I use discourses which, I hope, are accessible and liberating to the Aboriginal people I desire to represent, serve and place on the agenda. Indicative of this is the fact that not once has an Aboriginal person come up to me and said: 'Jackie, I can't understand a word you have said.' If they couldn't understand me, then for what and for whom would I be doing it? I would be guilty of marginalising my own people, myself among them. My *jingari* would be dead (life, spirit, purpose in life). This is my dilemma with regard to becoming an academic. Aboriginal people, like many 'others', are primarily visual language comprehenders.

Contrary to the prevailing myths, all Aboriginal people who have been socialised from birth in an Aboriginal community are from a non-English-speaking background. Our mother tongue is Aboriginal English. I sure as hell don't speak in public as I do at home and in private. A number of years ago, myself and eleven other Tiddas were instructed that before we had any possibility of getting a Letter to the Editor published in an international feminist journal we would need to rewrite it so that (mainly Anglo feminist) academics could understand it.[1] Now that's a role reversal if ever I heard one! We had made it so simple it alienated them! However, we stood our ground on principle and solidarity and never put pen to paper, and were published one long year later.

Hence this is a plea of sensibility not to speak in riddles, for those of us who are caught in the crossfire of being non-Anglo and in the public domain, when addressing our own mob.

At 4 am I went to bed exhausted but relieved.

P.S. This has been cleared by the T.E.C. (Tidda's Ethics Committee).

White Apron, Black Hands: Aboriginal Women Domestic Servants in Queensland[1]

A collaboration between Lel Black, Leah King Smith and myself produced an Aboriginal women's domestic service exhibition. I wrote the text and catalogue (from which this article is taken) and interviewed the women who told their stories so eloquently. Their oral histories were recorded as part of the history that needs to be rescued, told and recorded for prosperity. A huge launch took place at the Brisbane City Council Art Gallery in 1994 with friends and family members of the women interviewed in attendance. I still recall their faces as they stood with pride and dignity finally being commemorated for their role in the labour force – a long-overdue recognition.

———

In the first half of this century it was commonplace for young Aboriginal women and men to be contracted out to those white people 'in need' of domestic and stockwork help. Most Aboriginal people never had a choice about which white people they would be sent to work for. For those Aboriginal people living on missions and reserves, the standard procedure was to send a trooper or native policeman, acting on orders from the reserve superintendent, to the homes of prospective employees. The officers would instruct the parents of the young women and men to have them ready for the morning train to an unknown destination. Thus at the average age of twelve or thirteen their work began on pastoral stations, under the control of government officials, doctors and policemen and whoever required their services.

There appear to have been two distinct working experiences in the domestic service sphere: those of the women who lived on missions, reserves and settlements 'under the Act' and those who, usually through their parents, were exempted from the Act. Most of this latter group of women were not born on missions or reserves or did not live or associate with people on them. Exemption came at huge personal cost. Often exempted people were not allowed to see or mix with their own relations. Pearl King (nee Rigby) states that when her father became exempt from the Act he had to move and could not have any connection with his family. As a result she only knew one brother. The legislation succeeded in its intention to divide and rule the physical and psychological lives of Aboriginal people. Janet Daisy adds that she was 'brainwashed' into believing that white was best and that to become assimilated was the best thing for her.

Aboriginal women's working accounts depict a long and busy day, in which they were required to perform many and varied tasks. Among the main ones were cleaning, washing and ironing, and other tasks such as drawing water, butchering livestock and chopping sugar cane were requested when there was a shortage of workers. In more isolated areas, Black women performed a wider range of jobs than their European counterparts: mustering cattle, droving, acting as shepherds, road and fence building and repairing, and other hard manual labour jobs.

Fortunately, some women were able to choose their jobs. For instance, Irene Egert, who had previously worked as a domestic at the Peel Island leprosy colony, said she 'couldn't come at the bar work' which was offered to her at the Indooroopilly Hotel. Aboriginal domestics worked long hours, and their little leisure time was taken up with rest, outdoor stimulation, walking and horse-riding, reading, writing letters back home and other personal chores such as washing.

The irony of all this is that most Black women are grateful for the experience of their domestic service years. Some say that it gave them good training for their future lives with their husbands and children. It was not always true though that white women taught Black women how to do everything, as Maggie Ross, an Aranda woman, vehemently tells us:

> Yeah, they (white women) myall, bloody myall, can't cook a bloody lizard, can't make a bloody johnny cake, whole lot of 'em – nothing! Yes, all the native lady bin cookin' 'n showin' em ... (White woman) got to have a look (in a cookbook) first to cookem cake. Hahaha! ... But can't cook a bloody tucker, nothin'! ... All the (Aboriginal) woman bin washin' clothes, cleanin', cartin' water ... waterin' garden. White lady never do nothin'. Big Queen ...[2]

The Black domestic's entire day revolved around catering for the white family's needs, values and lifestyle. Rita Huggins was unable to keep her firstborn daughter Mutoo (Marion) with her when she was sent away to domestic service work. Instead Mutoo was left in the care of Rita's parents who then reared the little girl in the Cherbourg Aboriginal Settlement. Like other Aboriginal women, Rita was denied her own maternity while forced to wash, change babies' nappies and play with her white employer's children. A painful insult indeed. There are also many cases of Aboriginal women wet-nursing white children while 'the Big Queen' did other things.

Exempted women were privy to a far greater freedom of movement and received proper wages. Often employment was found through a white friend, an associate of the family or through word of mouth. Parents or contacts usually knew the people the girls would be working for and did not fear any harsh treatment. In fact, May McBride named two of her three children after some former employers and Lorna Bligh experienced a good relationship with her employers.

The Master and Servant Act (NSW) of 1845 was a feudal piece of legislation which made it an offence for employees to leave their place of employment without permission. Workers who did so were tracked down and brought back to face a thrashing or prison. It was these young people's first time away from home and family. Most were homesick and did not know the dire consequences of their actions.

Aboriginal women and girls throughout Queensland were sent to work in Brisbane. In order to facilitate the control of women in service, an institution known as the Aboriginal Girls' Home was established in 1903. The Home was set up for the purpose of receiving 'aboriginal and half-caste girls going to service, as a home for them changing from one position to another and a place where women passing through Brisbane could stay'.[3] From beginning to end, the home was plagued with problems. There were difficulties in even obtaining a suitable residence in Brisbane. When a house was located in West End, there was strong opposition from local residents and the mayor of South Brisbane.

During the nineteenth century, it was common for employers to pay Aboriginal workers in kind, by the provision of rations, blankets and other goods rather than by payment in cash. By the 1920s, cash payment had become common for seasonal or casual work, although not for other work.

In Queensland a different pattern prevailed. In addition to food and shelter, Aboriginal workers under the Aboriginal Acts were supposed to receive a wage. However, many still have never received a penny. Imagine the public outcry if this had been done to white people!

Examples of the severe treatment experienced by Aboriginal domestics are now fairly well documented in the autobiographical and other historical writings of Aboriginal women themselves, for instance Glenys Ward, Jennifer Sabbioni and myself.[4] Marnie Kennedy sums up the dismal situation:

> When the whites had pounded every bit of our lifestyle, culture, language and our identity out of us, which left us a mass of bruised and broken humanity, we were signed on and sent out to slave for the white man.[5]

The word 'slave' is synonymous with domestic service testimonies. The types of treatment ranged from cruel and barbaric to generally kinder, but never egalitarian, indicating a clearly oppressive relationship between Black and white, servant and boss/mistress.

Domestics even had to address the children of their employers with the title of 'Master' or 'Miss'. People were gripped by a racist mythology which claimed that Blacks were inferior and were poor workers who needed to be firmly controlled by the 'supreme race', no matter what ages they were. This ideology had to be upheld at all times.

Despite the maltreatment and other hardships faced by Aboriginal women, their resilience and determination can never be erased. It seems that they have never lost their identity, strength and independence, despite all the injustices and obstacles that have hindered them. The recollection of their lives is recalled with humour and frankness.

Unfortunately the women who are no longer with us cannot tell us what it was like for them. We can only surmise that their stories depicted a life of subjugation and exploitation too.

Respect versus Political Correctness

Some writers and social scientists have asked me about their ethical concerns when writing about Aboriginal people. In fact they asked me so often that I thought I'd better draw up a formula to assist in their dilemmas and to save myself from repeating it so often. It is so much quicker when one can say, 'Now read this.' My article is however by no means the perfect prescription. Human error can enter into every judgement and the way I view my world is not the same as the next person. To all those who presumably represent us this essay (written in 1993) was a plea that the process is crucial to the best outcomes.

—

The best books written about Aboriginals by non-Aboriginals are by those who have some relationship and friendships with Aboriginal people themselves. Having a respect for and knowledge of Aboriginal culture, history and social issues and what was happening to Aboriginal people in the era being written about is imperative to how one writes the Aboriginal characters and situations. It may seem a tall order for some, but ask any non-Aboriginal writer who has had this experience. Cultural and social barriers can be transcended and a long-term meaningful liaison usually occurs between the parties. Sometimes it changes a person's perspective on life.

One word of caution though – don't expect Aboriginal people to easily welcome you into their world. Some of us will be more open and tolerant than others. There is a long history of violence, mistrust, guilt and fear that cannot be erased overnight. Know when you are becoming an intruder rather than an accomplice. Do some homework first. Read books, watch films, do Aboriginal Studies courses. You should never expect Aboriginal people to do all the education because it's unfair and a personal drain – and we never get paid for it (*gammon* – only joking). If there is trust, respect and genuine interest, one will possibly get past the first encounter and continue a dialogue.

With the new term 'political correctness' flaunted in everyday discourse, one often gets accused of being 'oversensitive' when objecting to outdated and offensive words. Many Aboriginal people have been speaking and writing about how we prefer to define ourselves for years prior to the intervention of political correctness. One can only hope the right-wing backlash does not continue for long.

Some non-Aboriginal writers appear to have a dilemma about whether to use the horrific terms which my people have been insulted with for years – unpalatable words like 'boong', 'abo' and 'coon' for instance. While they have a widespread and common usage with non-Aboriginals, we never use those insidious terms among ourselves, even in the context of humour, because of their racist assumptions.

To attempt to find similar examples which whites would find hurtful is to no avail. Words that spring to mind are 'motherfucker' and 'whitetrash'. But unfortunately, all our insulting words about whites are too soft, for instance 'migaloo' and 'gubba' which virtually mean ghost. Our people have been too tolerant, it appears, due to the great humanness of our society.

In the case of words like 'wog' or 'dyke' which are becoming increasingly 'respectable', it is for the people who are of those groups to re-invent and re-ascribe the word to themselves, not for any outsider. I cannot see the day coming when Aboriginal people will use the above-mentioned derogatory words as victory symbols. They are not historical words, they are cretin words.

Of course language is not static. The nineteenth and twentieth century terminology, like 'octroon', 'half-caste' and 'full-blood' and the ones previously mentioned, will soon become obsolete. We can be sure, however, there will be new ones to take their place.

While there has been a popular revival of Dreamtime/creation stories in children's literature, it is my firm opinion that these should be exclusively written by Aboriginal people. Much information written about Aboriginals by non-Aboriginals has been patronising, misconstrued, preconceived and abused. We've had so much destructive material written about us that we must hold together the fabric of the stories which created us. Out of all the material written about, for and by Aboriginal people, this is perhaps the most sensitive genre. We never refer to these stories as 'myths' because how can the Bible be a myth?

If jungaris or little hairy men or any other Aboriginal spiritual characters are written about, they must emanate from the right source, region or people to whom those stories belong. Jungaris are not found everywhere throughout this country and appear for specific purposes only with rituals attached to them. Some writers treat these characters with the same applicability and generality as they do ghosts, witches and gnomes. One playwright told me he 'just put them in for effect', not realising the protocols involved. I prefer that people don't write about them at all rather than with this colourisation and tokenism.

Romanticising about a pristine Aboriginal past or present can also be patronising. Aboriginal culture has adapted and changed under drastic circumstances over the past 206 years. Pretending that Aboriginals are something they are not is not helpful. Little Black

Princess, piccaninnies, and egalitarian Black and white relationships and friendships are fictions.

We live in a society now where only 20 of our original 3,000 languages have been preserved. We are so decimated by the process of colonialism that it is difficult to reconstruct an intact Aboriginal past. The problem with some writers is that they have 'made up' what they don't know about. This dangerous methodology only serves to alienate socially aware readers and those people whom it is meant to benefit.

A recent stereotype which white Australia has applied to Aboriginals is that we are a spiritual people. Although most of the spirituality has been knocked out of us through our daily survival, Aboriginal people are still expected to perform as if they are deeply spiritual. This is especially necessary for the new-ageists' agenda.

Perpetuating stereotypes and racism are the worst forms of paternalism that writers can indulge in. Sometimes this is done subconsciously or unknowingly. However, even when this paternalism is pointed out, there is that sharp defence we all feel as writers about our 'holy' works. An example of stereotyping is writing about an Aboriginal student as a low-achiever. How about telling that to my Year 12 nephew at Marist College Ashgrove who is in the top ten of his senior year. It is vital to depict positive role models, otherwise Aboriginal children don't have much to look forward to in life let alone in reading.

There are many ethical issues which need to be considered when writing about Aboriginal people. The following formula has proved to be quite successful when dealing with Aboriginal issues:

(a) Detached observer status is not advisable. Consult with the relevant Aboriginal organisations and individuals before beginning the project.
(b) Research relevant literature, films and audios associated with the project.

(c) Keep Aboriginal people informed and advised, and where possible provide regular updates.

(d) When the first draft of the work has been completed, take it back to the Aboriginal community and people for their approval and for them to vet.

(e) The material needs to empower not disempower Indigenous people.

This may all appear complex and unnecessary but really it is simple and makes good sense. These cross-checks may prove helpful in depicting Aboriginal people as both victims and survivors and in reclaiming their rightful place in Australian society. It might also provide a more equitable representation and a long overdue reconciliation.

The Great Deception: Working Inside the Bureaucracy

I have believed in the old adage that when one door closes another one opens. In terms of my working experience (unlike Baamba in Bran Nue Dae) *I've had plenty and varied. It's as if my path is beset by one of the old people, directing me here and there, 'Do this,' 'No, that's not right for you just yet.' The seeming risks taken always pay off even now, to my joy. Written in 1995, this piece speaks of my frustration with bureaucracy although it was a good learning time.*

—

After leaving school in 1972 I was content to obtain employment wherever I could. Being an impressionable 16-year-old, the world seemed my oyster – I had clothes, a car, a boyfriend and my choice of jobs. Those were the good old days when jobs were plentiful, especially for a young and enthusiastic Black woman. The Commonwealth Employment Service (CES) had just begun a policy of recruiting Aboriginal people and Torres Strait Islanders into the workforce and other places where we dared not go. Consequently I ended up in the Australian Broadcasting Commission (ABC) which is a statutory authority but a bureaucracy just the same, tied down by rules and regulations and a hierarchical pecking order. Unbeknown to me, but not surprisingly, I was right at the bottom of the imperial pile – an

Aboriginal female Typist Grade 1. I never knew anything about class then, but I had had many experiences and was mature in the area of racial inequality and discrimination.

The money in those days was absolute heaven. My $75 per fortnight went a l-o-n-g way – from paying my Mother board to raging a Saturday night away. They say the more you earn the more you spend, and it couldn't be truer in my case. I just loved paydays and would spend money wildly, being the extravagant Leo that I am. I also began to learn of the mysterious ways of the tax man. Wondering if it was all worth it, I guessed I'd have to play this game until my earning days were over.

All visibly Aboriginal people without exception are plagued by racism in some shape or form. The public service is not immune to it, and in fact, like most workplaces where people of different nationalities mix, there was a festering intolerance to difference. This intolerance often reared its ugly head against me, but I recall one vivid experience as if it was only yesterday.

I had arrived one morning to find two middle-aged co-workers huddled at a corner desk sniggering and laughing. The short, fat, bald ex-Vietnam veteran marched over to my desk as I began settling in for the day. 'Hey, Jackie, do you speak that boong language that they speak at West End?' he roared. Much to my surprise I roared back in a tirade of emotional and gabbled defence. Later that morning I was sent to the Boss' office where he told me not to be so sensitive.

The words I spoke now escape me, and although not coherent, the mere fact that I had responded so strongly shocked me more than my victim. From that point in my life I have never backed down when a racial slur comes within earshot. The only difference today is that I have become skilled at these kinds of conflict and am able to logically and vehemently articulate them, almost always coming out on top.

My time spent at the ABC laid the foundation for future jobs, and although I made long-lasting friendships there, I was passed over many times for promotion. I know in retrospect that it was because I never had the Caucasian characteristics of blonde hair and blue eyes like so many other young women of my age who would rise meteorically through the ranks. At that stage I did not understand racial-sexual oppression as clearly as I do now.

After six years' employment, the ABC did not offer any great challenges for me unless I wanted to type until I was sixty. Stick that! I had always felt a deep desire to work with and for Aboriginal people and it was soon time to get in touch with my ethical side. I resigned and moved to the public service Mecca of Canberra to embark on a career in Aboriginal Affairs.

I felt safe in the public service life. It offered security, excitement, money and now hopefully the satisfaction of being with my own people.

Unfortunately, life in Canberra was much the same as being in the ABC. It was far more official but with just as many white faces in the bureaucracy. But this time the whites seemed to be the experts in Aboriginal affairs and I went from working with whites who had never even spoken to a Murri to whites who knew everything (or thought they did). It was indeed a culture shock. The irony of the situation was that here I was attempting to become involved in Aboriginal affairs and there were no Aboriginal people around to get 'involved' with.

There were no Black role models to look up to. We were all relegated to lowly paid typist and clerical positions. My best friends again became the migaloos until I got a job with the Council for Aboriginal Development and National Aboriginal Secretariats. Now I started to see a few more Black faces and the role models began to appear, although unfortunately they were mostly Aboriginal men. Not that I have any problem with Aboriginal men being role models, but it would have been more powerful for me then as a young Black woman to see older Black women in leadership roles.

These were my early, informative years in the public service, which I recall were also my raging days, as socialising was more important than a career at that stage. 'What's a career?' I would continually ask myself. Despite the fun, I knew there was still a reserve of untapped potential hidden away inside me. In 1980 I received a promotion to Field Officer, Department of Aboriginal Affairs (DAA), Brisbane Area Office. This is what I had been searching for all my life. The opportunity had come where I could work among my people in a meaningful way.

I was lucky to be in the right place at the right time for many promotions which followed in the next couple of years, but by the tenth year of service I knew I was damn good (can you say that?). The 9 to 5 Protestant work ethic was clearly embedded and I loved doing what I was doing. So much, in fact, that I would gladly work fifteen-hour days four days a week without so much as raising a sweat. In retrospect, people were abusing my time and good nature and even though I worked at my bosses' levels, I wouldn't dream of doing anything else. After twelve years I had outgrown life in the public service and apart from establishing the DAA Women's Unit nothing offered a challenge any more. As they say in the westerns, 'it was time to mosey along'. And that I did – attending uni for five years and embarking on a writing career. My love is Aboriginal history and encouraging Murries to relate the 'other side of the stories'.

So having told my story I can reassess my time spent in the public service in a more objective way. Being too close and on the inside colours the images of reality. Here I was a small cog in a huge machine believing I could change the system – as so many Blacks idealise, only to find out they are deceiving themselves. The great deception can only be changed by those in power, and as I write this I can still count the quota of Blacks in influential positions on one hand. So you continue to live a lie. I could not pretend any more.

Being a Black in the public service also means being the meat in the sandwich – between the group and the Department. Loyalties are severely tested, but if one is secure in one's identity all else will follow. Murries sense and know too well when you are gammon. Many view government Blacks as appendages of the departments they are employed with, rather than as individuals with their own personae. People would greet me with, 'Here comes DAA', and even today the mud sticks and Murries still label me with that tag. It's strange to think also that the Blacks who used to knock me are now sitting pretty up here in their own well-paid public servant jobs.

Black public servants also have to work three times as hard as a white person who can knock off at 5 or 6 pm and go home. Blacks are on call 24 hours a day. But then again there are two types of Abocrats – those who will and those who won't. The committed ones are worth their weight in gold and it is hard to gauge if they outnumber the drones or the suntanned public servants.

The things I most miss about the public service life are the air-conditioning (hence that other terrible term 'air-conditioned Blacks'), regular paydays, the odd drink at the pub, free phone calls and photocopying, the artificial networking process, and little else, for I am free now. I never felt free in the public service, having always to answer to generally a master and sometimes a mistress. The hierarchical domination of the place stifled me, and my gravest insult came in 1984 when I had to report to an ignorant Anglo middle-class d—head about Aboriginal women's business. I didn't, and now I wonder if it was a case of having to resign to keep my sanity, perspective and pride. My workmates always seemed depressed working in that environment anyway, but the difference was that they were trapped by mortgages, cars, loans, debts and marriages and I wasn't, so it was easier for me to make my escape.

Having said all this, I don't regret my years spent in the public service, for it taught me many things – like how to fight racism, write reports and drive a Z car and that there is more to life than being a bureaucrat. My creative side has overtaken my career ambitions and I know now that it would take a hefty offer to lure me back to a full-time public service position. As I have said, I am free of the great deception.

The Mothering Tongue

In 1995 Mother and I were speaking at the International Feminist Book Fair in Melbourne. She was not very well at the time, her health was slowly declining, but she was in as good spirits as she could muster. Those closest to her were in denial about her health and we all expected her to live until one hundred. So I wrote this piece to cheer her up and tell her how much she meant to me.

—

I am a privileged Aboriginal woman. I am privileged because:
- I have grown up with my family
- I have never been taken away
- I have been socialised into believing that the dignity of the human spirit is tied up in my Aboriginality
- I have a Mother like Rita.

The mothering tongue has nurtured and guided my life through the mountainous walls of prejudice, suffering, innuendo and pain. For many Aboriginal women, our Mothers, Grandmothers, Sisters, Aunties and cousins are our buffer zones against, and our sanctuaries from, the hostile world which awaits us. This is a given, a right, a gift – the lore.

The mothering tongue is one which speaks from the hundreds-of-years' experience of degradation, segregation and near annihilation.

She speaks of the hardships, the failed relationships and the friendships as much as she speaks of the isolationism, racism and paternalism. But more, she is proof of the enduring spirit of Aboriginal women.

Without her, I would never do what I do today and be who I am today.

But no, I've never had the perfect relationship with my Mother – as we all haven't, I suspect. The mothering tongue has also meant the 'fighting with our tongues', an expression my Mother is particularly proud of and which I understand full well, often being the recipient of this very precise form of oral tradition which she has perfected ... to a T! Little girls do grow up, however, and there is much more versatility and acrobatic exchange these days in the dialogue.

The mothering tongue smooths the waters although at times they seem like tidal waves. She tells me when to relax and to slow down when the pace is frenetic, even if I never do. Most Aboriginal women do too many things, too much, too often. Aboriginal women are always being stretched to the limit to speak, write, perform and educate; and there's just not enough of us to meet every demand and expectation. Consequently, we end up doing the lot and saving very little time for ourselves and our needs.

The mothering tongue is the political, even though she doesn't think she is! Being an advocate for her people, she has to tell a history which has been denied to her through colonialism. She is being forced to remember when once she was forced to forget. It's not easy piecing the pieces together in the Murri woman's jigsaw. There are pieces for oppression, exclusion and barbarism, spaces for tolerance, acceptance and collaboration, but no room for denial, betrayal and inhumanity.

Being quite oppositional, the mothering tongue usually doesn't listen to the daughtering tongue. The mothering tongue does her utmost to go against the grain, or should I say the palate? In fact the unpalatables are usually brought up in some obscure or trivial way which is meant to have a meaningful impact but seldom does.

The daughtering tongue has to fight every inch of the way to be heard, which is why my Mother and I wrote our book together.

We have created our own spaces instead of me being told to 'Shut up while I'm talking and don't interrupt me' in that fond tone I've heard so many times before! In *Auntie Rita* we share my Mother's life in print. Our separate and distinctive voices record her life as viewed from our different spaces. The mothering/daughtering tongue allows a fluent and honest appraisal to be *mutually* articulated. Not only is *Auntie Rita* the first book by an Aboriginal mother and daughter, but it is unique in Aboriginal literature in its style and its discourse.

The story of struggle in *Auntie Rita* reveals the theme of survival. My Mother and I can only hope that it serves as an encouragement and reminder to all Aboriginal people that we still have much more to say and write about. There are more ears than ever before who want to hear it.

The mothering tongue has been both my salvation and my worst critic. We have gone through so many things together. She can read me like a book. She gives an abundance of praise and scorn accordingly. In one breath she's telling me she loves my earrings, and when she's really vindictive she tells me I'm the 'educated' one so I should know everything. I know she has hundreds of degrees over and above mine so that jars me and I usually let her have the last say.

My Tiddas (Sisters) all have stories about their mothers whether they're 'privileged' or not. I've been lucky in that mine has been an easier, in some ways, story to write than some. We can no longer hear the audible voices of our mothers who are no longer with us, but their voices still go on and remain with us in everything we do. We must do them justice in those ways that are our payback, tell our history and show our maternal legacy.

Yes, I have been angry about how my Mother was treated, how her life was dictated, how she was deemed invisible and worthless.

Her past is still her present as it is for all Blackfellas in this country. Deny it but the racism goes on on a daily basis. Reclaiming her stories and putting them in print addresses that emotion and will hopefully enhance Aboriginal history and, also, the writing being done by Aboriginal women like Ruby Langford Ginibi, Doris Pilkington and Pat Torres.

I unapologetically declare (and cannot translate the words into English) that I adore my Mother Rita even though she drives me crazy and vice versa. Without her, I and many others would be lost. She has a universal spirit which has survived through her resilience and humour, even when she and her people had been squashed and discarded by you know who. I dedicate this piece from *Auntie Rita* to her.

> I can just imagine what it must have been like in your time to be a single mother, not once but twice. Single motherhood is a hard and unrelenting job but the love for the child and all the worthwhile outcomes far outweigh the difficulties and courage needed to be alone.
>
> But as a single mother I have never been alone in the sense that you were. My anchor and the ability to do what I have to do, write, speak, travel, etc., comes from the fact that primarily you and Ngaire (Rita's daughter and Jackie's sister) share the responsibility of being a mother, carer and nurturer to John Henry (Jackie's son). It has been an unconditional act of love from both of you and I am so privileged to have been born into a culture and family so accepting of children and family.
>
> You were hardly more than a child yourself when you ran away from your family to a strange town where you only had two friends. Luckily Auntie Lear and Uncle Teddie were family, loved and cared for you as best they could and gave

you a desperately needed home in your time of need and your highest form of being.

I saw not only the loving way you welcomed my child into this world when I was confused and so unsure of myself and what the responsibility of being a mother might mean, but I also have seen the radiant way you welcome into the world all babies – of strangers as well as of the closest friends and relatives – and the way you welcomed particularly your grandchildren and great grandchildren. I understand so much more now.

I'm sure Mutoo (Rita's first child) realised you had to go to work. You had no choice in a life of domestic service. You were bonded and on contract. If you could have taken her on the stations, you would have done so, but in working from dawn to dusk there would have been no room for a small baby. Today we have the right to take our children with us to work. No one would dare take them from us.

For me, being a single mother has meant independence, freedom, choice, acclaim, unreserved happiness, status, and power over my own life, among other things. All of which you were never afforded. But things we shared in common were love, strength, stubbornness, struggle, shame in the beginning, absent fathers of our children, and, most importantly, being broke! Financial independence has to be worked at all the time, but still I have a far greater capacity to achieve this than you ever could have dreamed of in your day.

All I want to say to you is that it's okay. All your children and grandchildren love you, understand you and forgive you because being a single, Black and penniless pregnant woman in your time was your greatest test and punishment. [From *Auntie Rita*, pp. 47–48].

Kooramindanjie: Place and the Postcolonial

When I took this trip with my Mother to her 'born' country, as she affectionately called it, for the first time in my life I began to comprehend how many Aboriginal people have a deep, strong, spiritual attachment to their country. Their yearning for home lasts forever and is embedded and central to their lives long after they have been forcibly removed from their ancestral lands. In 1995, in the company of my boy, John, and my good friend Jane Jacobs, who recorded the story with me through another gaze, we discovered a new journey.

—

Kooramindanjie (Carnarvon Gorge) is 600 kilometres north-west of Brisbane in the sandstone tablelands of the Great Dividing Range of Australia. It is an oasis in the desert plains and Aboriginal people would travel many hundreds of miles to visit this place for water, food, shelter and ceremonies. It is the country of Rita my Mother and my maternal Grandmothers; it is Bidjara country.

Our people lived in this area for over 19,000 years (archaeologically speaking) in the maze of gorges, ranges and tablelands. Other tribal groups living around the area were Kairi, Nuri, Karingbal, Longabulla, Jiman and Wadja. However, since the government removals policy, descendants from these tribal groups are now scattered over wide areas of Queensland and northern New South Wales.

Non-Aboriginals misunderstand their cultural and ethical limitations in studying, researching and writing about Blacks. They must learn to step back in areas where they are not welcome (although they often think and presume they are), where they are intruders not accomplices. Otherwise, they can do great damage to Aboriginal people and our struggles, adding to the burden rather than alleviating it. Binney suggests that we cannot translate others' histories into our own – we can merely juxtapose them. Translation is detrimental to the integrity of one or the other historical tradition, or both. Rather than trying to understand the past on its own terms, some academics have sought to explain Aboriginal pasts in terms of a contemporary ethnographical present, which they confront but do not fully comprehend.

There are different experiences of the world, different bases of experience. If we begin our understanding as we actually experience the world, it is at least possible to see how we are located. What is known of the 'other' is conditional upon that 'other's' relative location. Whites must not ignore this by taking advantage of their privileged speaking positions to construct an external version of 'us' which may pass for our 'reality'. There must be limits to the ways our worlds are rewritten or placed in conceptual frameworks which are not our own.

Aunty Rita's born country

I was only a small child when we were taken from my born country. I only remember a little of those times there but my memories are very precious to me. Most of my life has been spent away from my country ... but I remember about the land I come from. It will always be home, the place I belong to.

My born country is the land of the Bidjara-Pitjara people, and is known now as Carnarvon Gorge ... There were huge cliffs and rocks, riddled with caves where many of my people's paintings were. Most caves and rock faces showed my people's stencilled hands, weapons and tools, and there were engravings here, too. Fertility symbols and the giant serpent tell us of the spiritual significance of the place. This place is old. My people and their art were here long before the whiteman came.

The caves were cool places in summer and warm places in winter, and offered shelter when the days were windy or when there was rain. They offered a safe place for the women bringing new life into the world. As had happened for my Mother and her Mother before her, going back generation after generation, I was born in the sanctuary of one of those caves. My Mother would tell us how my Grandmother would wash my Mother's newborn babies in the nearby creek, place them in a cooliman and carry them back to suckle on my exhausted Mother's breast ...

My Mother, Rose, had a Bidjara-Pitjara Mother known as Lucy Conway from the Maranoa River and a white father who was never married to her Mother. I never knew who her Father was. I don't know much about the contact my Mother had with whites. She had a whiteman's name, but she also had a tribal name, Gylma, and she spoke language and knew the old ways. My Father, Albert Holt, was the son of a Yurri woman known as Maggie Bundle and a white man, the owner of Wealwandangie Station. My Father was named after that man. Dadda was brought up on the station, away from his Mother's people. When he grew up he wanted to be with Aboriginal people, and started visiting the camps. He saw my Mother there and wanted to marry her. After that, he stayed in the camp with her, and then the children started coming.

One winter's night, troopers came riding through our camp. My Father went to see what was happening, and my Mother stayed with her children to try to stop us from being so frightened. One trooper I remember clearly. Perhaps he was sorry for what he was doing, because he gave me some fruit – a banana, something as unknown to me as the whiteman who offered it. My Mother saw and cried out to me, 'Barjun! Barjun!'

Dadda and some of the older men were shouting angrily at the officials. We were being taken away from our lands. We didn't know why, nor imagined

*what place we would be taken to. I saw the distressed look on my parents'
faces and knew something was terribly wrong. We never had time to gather up
any belongings. Our camp was turned into a scattered mess – the fire embers
still burning.*

*What was to appear next out of the bush took us all by surprise and we
nearly turned white with fright. It was a huge cage with four round things
on it which, when moved by the man in the cabin in front, made a deafening
sound, shifting the ground and flattening the grass, stones and twigs beneath
it. We had never seen a cattle truck before. A strong smell surrounded us
when we entered the truck and we saw brown stains on the wooden floor ...*

*The truck went on, travelling for two terrible days, going further south.
As if in a funeral procession, we were loud in our silence. We were all in
mourning. I can't remember what we had to eat or drink, or where we stopped
on the journey, and by the time we reached our destination we were numb
with cold, tiredness and hunger. And this new country was so different from
our country – flat, no hills and valleys, arid and cleared of trees.*

*It was Barambah Reserve (renamed Cherbourg in 1932) ... Here we
were separated from each other into rough houses – buildings that seemed so
strange to me then, with their walls so straight. Each family was fenced off from
the others into their own two little rooms where you ate and slept. The houses
were little cells all next to each other in little rows. A prison ... The place in fact
had its own gaol. A prison in a prison. There were white and Aboriginal areas.*

*No one had the right to remove us from our traditional lands and to do
what they did to us. We were once the proud custodians of our land and now
our way of life became controlled by insensitive people who knew nothing
about us but thought they knew everything. They even chose how and where
we could live. We had to stay in one place now while the whiteman could
roam free.*

Dis-place-ment

During the late 1920s Rita and her family were rounded up by the
troopers and sent on the back of a cattle truck to the then Barambah

Aboriginal Reserve, later known as Cherbourg. Rita reminisces about the time of traditional Aboriginal existence in a manner which most people would find beautiful. Her stories are glimpses of a pristine past prior to the white invasion. She tells me:

My Mother would make soap from the leaves of a tree and unfortunately for us there was no excuse not to take a bogey. Goanna fat was used for cuts and scratches on bare feet and limbs as well as soothing treatment for aches and pains. Eucalyptus leaves for coughs and bark for rashes and open wounds. Witchetty grubs for babies' teething while charcoal was used for cleaning teeth. Bush tucker also thrived in this environment and we were never left with empty bellies. The men would go hunting for kangaroos, goannas, lizards, snakes and porcupines with their spears, boomerangs and nulla nullas while the women gathered berries, grubs, yams, edible roots, wild plums, honey and waterlilies with digging sticks. Children always accompanied the women as there was less likelihood that animals would run away when disturbed. The creeks supplied an abundant and rich source of fish – jew, yellow belly, perch and eels. [From her book *Auntie Rita*]

While my Mother recalls an idyllic Carnarvon Gorge her memories efface a history of an opposite kind; the bloody massacres which occurred not only here but right across the continent. They were acts of violence intended to demonstrate white supremacy and power.

The perpetrators were seen as heroic pioneers who had entered into the place they saw as 'wild' but which we called home. Their quest was to tame the 'natives' and possess the land. Their greed cost my people dearly. There was only one thing they could do with us – get rid of us completely so they would not have anybody else to consider. Then our tranquil home could become their fortresses and their recreational areas. They did this through force and theft, by poisoning flour and waterholes, burying Blackfellas alive, tying them to trees for shooting practice, and much more. The scarcity of white women in colonial times meant that the colonisers sexually exploited Aboriginal women. The result was rape and 'half-caste' children who were usually disowned by their white 'fathers'. The conquerors killed Aboriginal dogs and game, they dispossessed us of our hunting grounds and destroyed our sacred sites.

In 1857 the Jiman people whose country bordered Carnarvon Gorge retaliated against the invaders. They attacked and killed those who lived and worked on the Fraser homestead of Hornet Bank Station. This acted as the catalyst for what became known as the six months 'little war' which was waged against the Jiman and other Aboriginals in the Central Queensland area by white vigilantes. Many Aboriginal people – men, women and children – in the area were shot down as punishment for the killing of the Fraser family. The reprisals developed into an uncontrollable rage and resulted in the wholesale slaughter of innocent human lives. No effort was ever made to bring the white murderers to court. The killings and mutual hatred created during this period went on long after, and all over Australia.

The people of my Mother's generation display a profound lack of bitterness about their lot, something which I find both frustrating and amazing. This trait has often polarised old and young Aboriginals. It has encouraged many of my generation to become active in fighting the continuing injustices against our people.

We were once the proud custodians of our nation and then our way of life was irreversibly shattered by the controlling hand of colonialism. Aboriginal people could not choose how or where to live again. Under the powers of the *Queensland Aborigines Protection and Restriction of the Sale of Opium Act 1897* we were dictated to by government officials and told to stay in one place. If we wanted to go off the reserves set aside for us we had to get clearance from the reserve officials. This clearance was known as a permit and the system was standard practice in Queensland from late last century until the 1980s. It was only through the permit system that we were allowed 'freedom' from the reserves. We became like prisoners or occasional tourists in our own country.

Reclaiming place

Returning to my Mother's 'born country' complemented my own sense of identity and belonging, and my pride in this. It was important to me that we made this trip together, as she had been insisting for quite some time, pining for her homelands. We shared a special furthering of our mother–daughter bond during this time, although we argued incessantly about nothing, as usual, or, as she calls it, 'fought with our tongues'. I began to gain an insight into and understanding of her obvious attachment and relationship to her country and how our people cared for this place long before the Royal Geographical Society or park rangers ever clapped eyes on it. The way my Mother moved around, kissed the earth and said her prayers will have a lasting effect on my soul and memory, because she was paying homage and respect to her ancestors who had passed on long ago but whose presence we could both intensely feel.

This was our place, my sense of becoming. The land of my Mother and my maternal Grandmother is my land too. It will be passed down to my children and successive generations, spiritually, in the manner that has been carried out for thousands of years. As Rita's daughter, I not only share the celebration and the pain of her experience but also the land from which we were created. Like most Aboriginal people it is my spiritual and religious belief that we come from this land, hence the term 'the land my Mother'. This land is our birthing place, our 'cradle'; it offers us connection with the creatures, the trees, the mountains, the rivers, and all living things. This is the place of my Dreaming. There are no stories of migration in our Dreamtime stories. Our creation stories link intrinsically to the earth. This is why place and land are so important to us, regardless of where and when we were born.

The High Court Mabo decision of 1992 and the subsequent Native Title Act will attempt to rectify some of these injustices through the new land claim process. Claims are already being prepared on behalf of the Bidjara people for the Carnarvon Gorge area. Five other clan groups may also lay claim to it, as this place was used by a number of groups for ceremonial purposes. Tensions are mounting between the Aboriginal Traditional Owners and interest groups, pastoralists, National Parks and Wildlife Service, and of course the white experts. Decisions made by the Aboriginal Land Claims Tribunal will need to consider the concerns of all interested parties and not just Aboriginal concerns. Any claims we Bidjara people make to this country under the provisions of the new Native Title Act will have to counter the myth that there are no Aboriginal people for this place. The claims we as Aboriginal owners of this land can make are tainted by dispossession and its violence on our memories. Like Rita, other Elders will now be pressured to remember their childhood memories of their place to help prove our association with this country. Not so long ago the protectionist and assimilationist policies of the day pressured our Elders to deny and forget. How ironic it is that now every detail must be recalled and told and that this remembering and this telling is now honourably encouraged and documented and forms the basis for land claims being won or lost. History finds a way of reinventing itself for Aboriginal people, for better or for worse.

In conclusion, I return to the early tourists. Their desire for tourist pleasure was always shadowed by the memory of violence. Mrs Hamlyn-Harris was one of the first women to go on a Royal Geographical Society Carnarvon expedition. She wrote a series of poems about this place as a tribute to the intrepid leader Danny O'Brien. In one of her poems, simply entitled 'Carnarvon Gorge', she contemplated the history that led to her coming to my place.

Yes, what have we done?
The past is dead by our own hand. The olden race is gone.
They are but ghosts, those spirits of the wind and trees,
That sigh such doleful threnodies!
We of To-day by duty bound must wake
And silence them with Joy's sweet laughter ringing,
And children's voices singing!
We must arise, and of this primal playground make
A resting place for toiling families of the drought-stricken west
Needful of Nature's healing and of rest.
Thus shall we at last
Make humble expiation for the past.

Turning Kooramindanjie Place into Queensland's 'biggest picnic ground' has not made 'humble expiation' for the past.

Oppressed but Liberated

My university days were most enjoyable. It was there that I discovered how much I loved to write and I was one of those students every other student hated. I would get my assignments in three weeks in advance and to add insult to injury I never asked for one extension in the whole five years there. Some of my best writing was done there. Thinking back, I believe writing was so important to me because it was a liberating experience. Issues of race, class and gender began to appear much clearer. This was written in 1995.

—

For many years now my activism in Aboriginal affairs has included a variety of inescapable experiences, some as object and some as subject where feelings of powerlessness and empowerment have directed the situation against and in favour of Aboriginal people.

And while racist-sexual oppressions are experienced simultaneously, it is very difficult at times for a woman to separate out the bits of oppression she experiences and decide whether she experiences each bit because of her gender, class or race. However, in the case of Aboriginal women the overwhelming evidence and experience points to the fact that we remain discriminated against because of our race rather than our gender, particularly by non-Aboriginals. Racial discrimination over and beyond sexual discrimination is the prejudice most cosmetically apparent Aboriginal women experience. The following story illustrates this as the segregations of race and gender become clearer.

The Diploma of Aboriginal Education instilled in me a positive and enthusiastic attitude to teaching. Prior to seven weeks of teaching prac in the Northern Territory, I was looking forward to the challenge of teaching in (what I was led to believe was) an Aboriginal school. I felt strongly motivated to get started.

After many hours of travelling to the bush, this motivation turned to despair on my first meeting with some members of the school staff who had arrived at the motel to pick up our excess luggage. As the door opened, to their amazement there I stood. I had seen that look so many times before, the look that attempts to belittle one's confidence, that asks, 'Hey, what gives you the right to be here?' or says, 'So you're the student teacher and – you're Black!' Only Aboriginal people know what it feels like to be degraded in this way, to feel the taunt of racist jibes.

As I boldly stared back, one woman, as if to cover up a guilty party's embarrassment, kindly informed me that 'the children will be glad to see you – no offence of course love – but someone of the same colour – you know what I mean.' I replied that I was indeed looking forward to acting as a role model for these children. Intuitively I predicted that this would set the scene for the next seven weeks. However, nothing could have prepared me for what lay in store.

There were two camps in the small non-Aboriginal community: the racist and the non-racist elements. Surprisingly, the people who I thought would be overtly racist and who Aboriginal people would feel most defensive about – the police and their families – ironically became strong allies in the end. I suspect having had the opportunity to teach the senior policeman's two daughters for almost half my teaching prac contributed to the goodwill felt between us.

Ablaze in green and gold Bicentennial colours, the school was ethnocentrically Anglo in its administration and operation. Responsibility for formal education rested with teachers who were not accountable as employees to the Aboriginal community. I was initially allocated to a married, conservative, middle-class supervising teacher who told me that she was there to make her 'gold mine' and then leave. Her lack of interest in Aboriginal education was quite evident, claiming that after six years at the school she could not speak one word of the local Aboriginal language.

It soon became apparent that I was teaching at a school which was blissfully ignorant of the cultural differences between Aboriginal people and non-Aboriginal people and which had chosen to 'safely' teach the children using assimilationist methods. This grated on my deeply-held beliefs of sensitively integrating Aboriginal education within the white system.

I was forewarned that the style of the school was unlike ordinary 'bush' schools. Being the largest building around for miles its squeaky clean image belied its oppressive teaching of Aboriginal children. Everything I hated about the Anglo treatment of Aboriginal values and lifestyles as unimportant was to be found here. In the Australian education system Aboriginal children learning at school are taught an entirely different set of values from the ones which they may learn in their Aboriginal home. For example, to tell another child the answer to a question is 'sharing' that information, while it is perceived as 'cheating' by Anglos. The Aboriginal children therefore can become cultural misfits who cannot effectively relate to either Aboriginal society or white society.

I would not have even attempted to plan a geography lesson with the students as, like the Bob Hawke treaty, it would introduce 'pie in the sky' for the victims, who had not had sufficient cross-cultural and educational sensitivity thrust upon them to enable them to cope with such airy-fairy concepts. Besides, what could a mere urban mortal like me teach these children about the land? Aboriginal cultural knowledge about and expertise in climate, relief, soil and vegetation was far superior to European knowledge. Aboriginals knew all the available edible plants, animals and insects. In the northeast, some 240 species of edible plants were known and a further 90 species of molluscs were common knowledge. In north central Australia from five to nine different climatic seasons were recognised, along with times when supplies of game and plant food varied, and when certain parts of tribal areas were more attractive for occupation than others. They were the true experts and it was presumptuous of me to assume otherwise. The white education system has much to learn from Aboriginal people; indeed, white Australia should be looking to Aboriginal expertise in describing the nature of geography.

In fact, nothing much had changed since I went to school some sixteen years ago. As one perceptive young teacher pointed out, 'You might as well be teaching in suburban Sydney as out here if this is how Aboriginal education is being taught today.' Constantly I felt myself identifying so well with these students, drifting back to my primary school days when I was one of about three Aboriginal children in a class dominated by white children. However, even though the white children at the school here were in the minority (95 per cent Aboriginal, 5 per cent white) I couldn't help feeling that the whole system and style of teaching was geared directly to the white children rather than to the Aboriginal majority. If the reverse situation to mine and that of many Aboriginal children in other country and urban schools had occurred, what a difference it would make, for now we would be witnessing a 90 per cent success rate in Aboriginal education.

When a system works only for a few and not for the majority, it is the system that is at fault, not the people for whom it is offered. From an Aboriginal point of view, the system had failed and had a lot to answer for in the teaching of Aboriginal students. The system as it was operating at the school created the alienation of Black children from the culture of their parents, and it assumed that European culture was superior to Aboriginal culture, and hence avoided relating to the latter. The children and their parents were never consulted about what and how they would like to be taught, therefore making the process entirely white ethnocentrically determined.

Children are conditioned into accepting the 'culture' of the powerful and dominant white society and that the white way of understanding and doing things is the 'right' way. The European approach to education is based on competitiveness by way of achievement, topping the class and striving for academic excellence.

In terms of achievement and competitiveness Europeans have a totally different concept to Aboriginal people of what these words mean. Individual achievement is important to Europeans but is a cultural barrier to Aboriginal people, as kinship and social networks dictate an Aboriginal person's life and make it impossible for an Aboriginal to excel unless she or he assures their community that it is being done for them and not for the individual. Similarly no one has convinced me that competitiveness is inherent in Aboriginal culture, as traditional Aboriginal society was egalitarian. This extends into the contemporary scene where Aboriginal 'leaders' and achievers are constantly pulled down by their community for their seeming competitiveness and standing 'beyond' the group.

I can draw parallels between my twelve years in the public service and what life is like as a teacher in a school of this type. A small cog in a huge machine. People are always insisting that you can change the system from within, but from my personal experience this is not the reality. Sure one may gain a few wins here and there but nothing which radically alters the institution's philosophies or policies. You are always working within an oppressive framework. No, I could not endure several more years of that, as one can actually become deluded that you can 'change the system'.

The whole teacher-training experience set me back 200 years. Just when an Aboriginal person feels that wonderful and positive things are happening for the Aboriginal race and that finally Australian society is coming together to accept Aboriginal people, a glaring example of archaic and colonial attitudes stands entrenched and affects the very psyches of the users and facilitators of the country's educational institutions.

Aboriginal people believe that the challenge in education today is to prepare their children to be able to maintain their own cultural identity as well as functioning in the wider Australian community to their own and to their people's advantage. Therefore co-existence without inhibiting identity is the right Aboriginal people seek.

For this reason I now believe my skills would be better spent on concentrating on 'white Australia as a whole' rather than on isolated Aboriginal children who would never stand a chance in mainstream society. My conviction is even deeper that Anglo adults need educating about Aboriginal people far more than Aboriginal children need to receive whitefellas' education in this country.

My disappointment with my teaching experience directed my further studies into another area which before had held little relevance – Women's Studies. History has always been my field of study, so it was interesting to combine the two subject areas for postgraduate purposes. It also allowed relief from the stagnation of a disastrous year.

My personal motivation in pursuing Women's Studies was to investigate the avenues whereby Aboriginal and non-Aboriginal women may form alliances where we might tackle the issues of all kinds of oppression together. It has always been my belief that it is through the women of a society that social change can be more rapidly achieved. My grounding as an Aboriginal woman is the essence of my life and career.

To be honest, the theoretical debates of Women's Studies did not set my world on fire, but they did equip me with aspects of knowledge already familiar to me as a Black woman. Attempting to apply them within my own cognitive framework did prove difficult at times. Like so many of my tertiary studies, an intermittent culture block played havoc.

The course content was advanced and the calibre of the lecturers and honours students was high – quite daunting in fact. However, no one was made to feel inferior or their contribution unworthy – a direct contrast to the majority of my four years undergraduate study. What occurred was the most supportive and memorable study program I'd ever undertaken.

Containing two 'misfits' – a Black woman and a migrant working-class woman – the class of three was nurtured by two of the most sensitive women I have ever had the privilege to meet. One had a background as a race relations historian, while the other, in her opinion, will always value the impact of that year and the learnings received. By the end of the year we were all experts in race and class issues in Women's Studies, for we two 'oppressed' but liberated women and our other colleague also became the teachers, creating a dynamic exchange of powerful woman politics.

I have never felt more comfortable with any group of white women than I did in the Class of '89. They all remain strong supporters and personal friends to whom I regularly confide my hopes and aspirations. This is where I began to find assistance and alliances outside my sphere of Aboriginal community connections and a previously small number of white women colleagues.

There is a continual expectation from white women that women of colour will educate them about racism. Quite frankly I resent this, although I find myself on a regular basis educating whites in some shape or form, whether as a conscious participant (for example as a panel member) or merely explaining why it is so about Blacks. But it is quite another matter for me to explain the history of racism, which is essentially to explain the coloniser's history of white people, and I do not own that one. It also insults my intelligence. Why set up the 'victim' to explain the injustices of that history to the people who have perpetrated it?

It is the responsibility of academics and educationalists to educate students about racism via the curriculum and other educational materials and through their teachings. There is no room for complacency by the educational providers and institutions of this country.

White women do not realise the advantages of the teachings and learnings of Aboriginal women. For many thousands of years we have been the benefactors of a wealth of knowledge and have learnt the strategies of survival and adaptability as well. At what price therefore are we willing to share this with other women? Not until we construct meaningful and anti-racist discourses which transcend the barriers and suspicions presently permeating between us.

It is not a simple matter of saying, 'Hey, let's start working together', as the mechanisms for doing so remain complex from the outset. As women we have all been subjected to divide-and-rule socialisation and racist and sexist ideologies. I argue strongly that for Aboriginal women the main oppressor remains the legacy of a racist inheritance in our country. Personally, I see racism and alcoholism and their manifestations as our greatest foes.

I believe there are some alliances which can be made between Aboriginal, non-English-speaking-background and Anglo-Australian women. However, at this time the majority of Aboriginal women who work with white women place them on the periphery of their experiences. Generally speaking, Black women prefer to be separate in our struggles, as more often than not our agendas are different.

There are also lines of accountability and responsibility to uphold. Questions which need to be asked are: Who has responsibility for what and whom? Who does what? Who takes responsibility for saying things for whom? Who does the saying and writing? Who gets the feedback and benefit? White women must realise 'where to get off' in the Aboriginal struggle. As the old saying goes, 'familiarity breeds contempt'. It may come to a point where it is no longer white women's business, so they should realise their limitations and let Aboriginal women do the rest.

Whites also need to realise where their responsibility begins and ends when collaborating with Aboriginals. For example, Aboriginal women must control the negotiations for the funding of their women's centres and so on. If Aboriginal women are not placed within this framework, enabling their own empowerment and taking responsibility for their own decisions, then that constitutes *maternalism* of the highest order.

White advisers are epitomes of the past. Where possible, Aboriginal people who are the keepers of their stories should write them down or enlist the assistance of another Aboriginal person to write them for them, thus minimising the sometimes very destructive material that is written for (and against) Blacks by both well-intentioned and unscrupulous white authors.

The arts and theatre are avenues of successful co-operation between Black and white women. I had the great fortune to be on stage with thirty Aboriginal and thirty non-Aboriginal women in *Is This Seat Taken?* at the Adelaide Festival Centre in November 1989. It was the first Australian production in which Black and white women performed together in a unique cabaret about women's lives. The show celebrated the hopes, fears, joys and sorrows of women from different cultures. Sketches, satire, song and dance were honestly performed confronting the contrasts and similarities in their differences. It ranged from the humorous to the deadly serious issues of land rights, prejudice and oppression.

Women from a wide range of backgrounds undertook the 'behind the scenes' technical, administrative and mechanical tasks. The exercise was a huge melting pot of diversity. Women began to work out their relationships to one another, their commonalities and differences and to treat those differences with fervour. Being associated with the show was one of my most explosive and heart-rending experiences. The strength of women working in solidarity like this was akin to the struggles that my fellow Aboriginal Sisters and I have participated in for so long.

The sensory impact and clear messages received by the audience will enrich their lives forever (as it did ours) and to see Aboriginal and non-Aboriginal women in egalitarian structures and discourses gives rise to great hope for the future. The warm and wonderful, sad and funny, hilarious and serious, hysterical evenings of theatre taught us all precious lessons.

And although this was an exciting event, the tragedy is that the majority of Aboriginal women will never see a play like this. There are not sufficient role models to indicate that Black and white women can work together to articulate and denounce racism, and to embark on constructive ways of dealing with our oppressions as Blacks *and women*.

It would be a fair statement to make that many Black women do not want to know about white feminism. I can't say I blame them. There are a multitude of reasons why this is so: (a) a closed women's movement which has never addressed the needs of Aboriginal women, (b) inherent racism within feminist circles, (c) white women's unfamiliarity with the process of colonisation and how it has affected all Aboriginal people (that is, the non-support of Black men and families), (d) elitism and subordination of subjects and objects, (e) exclusion of Black women by white women, (f) our struggle as Blacks first.

There is a retreat from the group-orientation of Aboriginal women (leaving one or two Black women continuing the struggle but working in isolation from other Black women) when we continue to be silenced by feminists who hide their heads in the sand because for them the issues are too complex, threatening and challenging.

The history and damage are such that I do not see Aboriginal women participating en masse in the slowly changing women's movement in Australia. Successes have come in individuals and small groups. However, as the challenges keep coming to dismantle the dominant forces, feminists should take heed in allowing Aboriginal women co-existence on our own terms and remember that we all, as women, have a stake in feminism and that white women don't 'own' it exclusively.

What we can do is be honest and straight-talking with one another. Feminists of privilege must be prepared to share their resources with those in less powerful places, for they are also tools against our oppression. Some will do this and some will not. However, the flower seedlings are beginning to sprout, although there will be many a thunderstorm yet before we can reap the harvest.

A new feminism must be constructed which is global and international – to embrace all issues of oppression and not just one of its manifestations. It must have open and egalitarian lines of communication and respect for the cultural diversity of oral and written forms of expression. Its revolutionary zeal should enable the freedom of all women – not just privileged white upper- and middle-class women but those Sisters who do not have access to the rights and pleasures of life enjoyed by so many. Until this is created we can never call each other 'Sister'.

Experience and Identity: Writing History

My love of history stems from my displacement as an Aboriginal person. Like most students I was fed on a diet of lies and invisibility about the true history of this country from a very young age. I hope the ignorance and prejudice are being corrected now throughout the school system. My son in Year 8 is learning much more about Aboriginal people and history than I ever did at school. I still worry though about how it is being taught, providing the exotic rather than the contemporary view. My experience and identity allow me to add an extra dimension to the craft of writing and teaching Aboriginal history. I try to explain that dimension in this interview done in 1996 with Judy Skene.

—

Do you think of yourself as an Aboriginal historian? Are there other identities that are more important to you?

I always say that I'm Aboriginal first ... Then I'm a mother, daughter, sister, aunt, cousin, woman, historian, etc. As I get older, the professional qualifications don't tend to really matter any more. Besides, labels piss me off. Certainly I am very proud to say that I am an Aboriginal historian because of what I do in terms of identity and reclamation. I'm an Aboriginal historian rather than an historian who happens to be Aboriginal. There's a huge difference there. Just think about it.

There are no other identities more important to me. The identity of a good human being is probably one to which I aspire, although my work as an Aboriginal cultural critic conjures up criticism from my own people as well as from whitefellas.

Have you found History a more useful tool than other academic approaches such as Anthropology, Women's Studies, Australian Studies etc.? Is History more open to appropriation?

I suspect, yes, because as a young schoolchild I, and so many other Australian people throughout the educational system, were taught lies. The study of history eradicated some of this and has personally proved to be a most helpful academic discourse. Is History more open to appropriation than those others? I think no more, no less than other disciplines. Probably it has been appropriated less than Anthropology because anthropologists have made some devastating impacts on the way that 'Aboriginality' has been constructed and Aboriginal people have been defined, and continue to be defined.

What are the differences between Aboriginal understandings of the past and white constructions of 'History'?

If we're looking at the very important oral tradition that Aboriginal people adhere to, then of course there are differences between Aboriginal concepts of the past and present. We get asked why we talk and live in the past all the time, but not to do so is to deny the fundamental right of our existence. It is also about shaping a future and living in our present. For instance, the tragic cases of deaths in custody are just another form of genocide. Discrimination in the workplace, in everyday life, is just another attempt at the genocide of my people. Reflections on the past for Aboriginal people is quite different to non-Aboriginal people. White constructions of history have been charged with this ethnocentrism which keeps us by and large excluded and marginalised, on the peripheries of existence.

What we are saying is, rather than be at the margins, we should be in the centre. Sometimes you think this message has been taken on board. At other times, you think, 'Why do I come here and talk to these people, why am I attending this conference when things just aren't improving? Why do I keep speaking out?' For example, I was at a writers' week recently where the theme was about the old and the new. It was okay for me to be a token representative of my people presenting an award, but when it came to Black authors participating on various panels, we were all excluded! This only happened a week ago. So I wonder about it all and I wonder if it's worth that particular fight when people are just not listening any more. I could hear them say, 'Oh, here she goes again!'

What are the problems of communicating oral traditions through a written academic medium?

They are two absolutely diametrically opposed forms of communication. Aboriginal oral traditions are expressed in very intense language. In my case, it's an urban Aboriginal English which I consider a language in its own right. Urban Aboriginal English as it is written in an academic medium faces the chance of being annihilated or subsumed into the dominant discourse, which doesn't offer us anything back in terms of our valid communication styles. So, when you are incorporating an oral tradition in writing, I think it should really be the oral method that stands alone, as the more or less valid interpretation. The written academic discourse can be used as a kind of a medium and an agency whereby the oral evidence is not tampered with, it's not filtered. It's very difficult to attempt to do that. I'd prefer to use italics or quotation marks when putting Aboriginal oral language into academic discourse. Sure, you can shape all the words around it but don't touch or tamper with that vibrant, rich and purposeful, natural, spontaneous language.

Can you elaborate on the oral history projects that you are currently involved in, such as the National Library project?

I'm involved with two oral history programs. The first one is a sort of 'Seven Up' [Seven Years On] program. Fellow historian Peter Read from the History department at ANU and I are working in conjunction with the National Library interviewing new and emerging Aboriginal leaders, Aboriginal or Torres Strait Islander people who we see as future leaders of this country. They have special qualities and abilities to make good leaders in the community. Now I know that's a value judgement but there are just some young people you know who stand out. I was privy to that experience while in Perth, where I met young Daniella Sabbioni, the daughter of Jennifer Sabbioni from Edith Cowan University. Daniella is in her first year of medicine at UWA. She has great commitment, and although she is young, she has a lot of mature ideas about how she'll work for the benefit of her people. Having a strong mother like Jennifer and a strong family really has influenced her life. I'm sure that where Aboriginal women such as myself and Daniella have had very strong role models in our mothers, then our struggle to eradicate the injustices to our people is a natural course. I wouldn't say it's easier because it's not easy, the whole process takes years – as I've learnt myself.

Peter and I will come back in seven years' time to interview people again to see what they are doing, if in fact they've reached their targets and goals. In Daniella's case, she will presumably be a doctor in seven years' time. We'll find out if Aboriginal affairs have changed, what they see as the role of other people in their lives, who their role models and inspirations have been. It's looking at the social history perspective, through oral text. I just think it's an honour to be doing this project.

For the other oral history project I'm currently a writer-in-residence in Adelaide working with the community there. I'm collecting oral histories, particularly with the theme of mother and daughter relationships. I've done a lot of oral history projects on the domestic servants' project 'White Apron, Black Hands', and for the 'Australia Remembers' program. I interviewed a lot of the old people who served in the war and their spouses.

In what ways can white historians acknowledge Aboriginal experiences when writing Australian history without being tokenist or imperialist? Do you find the work of any white historians useful?

The first 'real' history by a whitefella that I read was the book *The Other Side of the Frontier* by Henry Reynolds. I became elated after reading that book. It gave back a certain part of my own dignity which said that my people did fight for this country. We didn't just resist in a passive way as I was led to believe throughout my schooling days. Peter Read's written history has always been very acceptable to me. I think both those historians take the time to actually speak with Aboriginal people and, you know, come up to our level. So I think that the relationship between the historian and the Aboriginal people or community is very important.

I think that there are models now that have been shown to be non-tokenistic. It's about, I guess, not implying any ethnocentric viewpoints and preconceived value judgements in the writing of history. I know that's probably difficult for most people to do. History in this country has often been written by people who haven't even spoken to an Aboriginal person and I really object to that stuff, unless it is colonial history of course, because all the informants are gone now, those people can't defend themselves, nor can they give their own views.

Some very good examples of putting the Indigenous story within the framework of Australian history have been written by historians I collaborate with, like Heather Goodall and Tom Blake. Kay Saunders, Ray Evans and Lyndall Ryan have also done excellent work in this area.

What would you say to white historians who feel that they have no position from which to speak concerning Aboriginal people?

I think it is the responsibility of every historian, particularly if they are doing Australian history, to make some kind of commitment to the inclusion of Aboriginal people. Exclusion is a sorry story, but I would not want to be included if people didn't go about the process in a culturally appropriate way. It's up to people if they want to include or exclude us, that's their prerogative. However, I think to say that writing about Aboriginal people is too hard is a great cop-out. If historians feel they have no position to speak from concerning Aboriginal people then just don't do it rather than stuff it up. I'd prefer whitefellas, if they weren't sure of speaking about Aboriginal people, not to.

You have used the expression 'fighting with our tongues' in your work as a metaphor for the process of resolving differences of opinion. Do you think that Aboriginal and non-Aboriginal historians can engage in a similar process?

Sure, I think it's healthy to keep 'fighting with our tongues'. What I loathe is this silence when I write something. No one objects or comes back at me. I welcome healthy criticism of my work, but Aboriginal and non-Aboriginal historians haven't engaged with it much at all. It leaves your work in a vacuum not knowing what people really feel about it.

How do you think Aboriginal history should be taught within the context of tertiary education (e.g. its own course, part of Australian Studies, studies of Indigenous people)?

I think all of these are important: to have our own courses and to be part of Australian studies and to have Indigenous people as guest lecturers, teaching about cultural aspects of Aboriginal history. I guess I opt more for Aboriginal people being included as part of the Australian studies genre, because that is what we are.

Perhaps we might be able to break down some of the ghettoism that Aboriginal studies sometimes falls into within tertiary institutions, when it is deemed as half-baked, second-rate. So I would probably like to see it right across the board rather than falling into one particular slot.

In terms of what I would offer as advice to academics teaching, I've written on that subject in the *Australian Author* (vol. 26, no. 3, 1994, pp. 12–14). Also, Kay Saunders and I did a paper together at the Lilith Conference and that is about issues like consultation and negotiation with Aboriginal communities, about taking the information back to have it vetted and endorsed by Aboriginal people.

How is gender important to your work?

Gender has always been a focal point of my work and it will continue to be. It's definitely part of my identity, of being an Aboriginal woman. In the last few years I've placed less emphasis on gender. It sometimes detracts from my other work as an Aboriginal activist in terms of wanting to do something in the wider context. I'm not saying that I ever deny my womanhood. It's something that's obviously there, that's built in. But it's something that I probably want to move away from now, because I think I've written all I can in terms of gender politics, gender criticism, the white woman/ Black woman stuff, and criticisms of the white women's movement. If I ever enter into another critical essay, I'd really need to think hard because there are other things in my life now that are just as important, like social justice for all our people: men, children and women. I want to see how I can come to terms with a whole range of issues that aren't gender specific, but have the opportunity to reach and to liberate our whole race, rather than putting women's position first and foremost. Gender has always been an aspect of my work and will continue to be so.

In your writing, you appear to talk about feminists as a homogenous group (i.e. white, middle-class) which does not take account of critiques by people like bell hooks and Gayatri Spivak. Do you think that their theorising of race and gender is useful?

I think it's imperative to those societies in which they live. I don't believe that they haven't talked about feminists as being an homogenous group either, because bell hooks has said on many occasions 'white woman this'. She is one of my great role models in writing. She and Audre Lorde have been two of my inspirations of Black women's consciousness. hook's theorising of race and gender is brilliant. I've been accused of seeing white feminists as an homogenous group. My answer to that in this country is that until they start doing something about their own racism in relation to us and how this is inflicted upon us, then we will continue to see white feminists as one homogenous group. So I think when white women, white feminists give us some answers, some access and some privilege we don't necessarily have, and fix up their own racism, that's when I will start seeing people as liberal feminists, social feminists, radical feminists, whatever. I don't feel at all peeved that most Aboriginal people – that I know anyway – perceive feminists as being 'the white feminists'.

Is there any possibility of Aboriginal women emerging in the project of recognising differences within feminism?

Yes, I think that would be good and what a bloody good idea! Many Aboriginal women have no idea of what the differences are and certainly I'd be the first to roll up. It might give me a better idea of who they are out there. Having said all this, I have to say that – quote unquote – 'some of my best friends are white women'. The white women that I collaborate with have been very attuned to their responsibilities in this country of accepting their guilt and their racism and are attempting to do something with it. I appreciate the honesty and the integrity of those women, but furthermore, they don't stop at that. They also start accessing some of the harder stuff that I need to do in terms of Aboriginal people. This doesn't apply to Aboriginal women, it applies right across the board. I would probably be all for that, perhaps a workshop where we can get together and discuss these things, and reconciliation as well.

On the other hand, since about 1983 I've been grappling with how feminism relates to Black women as well as white women. I term anyone that is non-Aboriginal and not people of colour as white. I know that leaves out a lot of people but it's not for me to make up how they want to define themselves. It's up to them to come up with their own definitions. As an Aboriginal woman, I can identify with the problem of being defined by others and I feel very strongly about that. Now, in terms of Aboriginal women generally wanting to grasp hold of feminism, I think that our feminism has to be Aboriginal women's feminism rather than the white women's version. To me, white feminism has been just another colonial discourse of oppression for Aboriginal people. I believe it's everybody's responsibility to change that. If we all said everything is too hard then we should give up living, we should cut our breath off tomorrow.

However, the point I wish to get across is that Aboriginal women are still very comfortable within our own circles, within our own Aboriginal women's business. To me, at this stage it is just not on to make us join in a white women's movement. Aboriginal women have always had separate spheres and roles and I think it's a great survival mechanism, because we've been able to co-operate, to join together and remain intact. Sure, we have factions, all our factions play an important role in the struggle we're trying to pursue at any particular time. So where do we go from here? I think we go from here in small groups and individual ways.

For instance, we've just seen, last September, the great Feminist

Bookfair in Melbourne, where Indigenous women were incorporated onto the wider committee, yet there wasn't even a space provided where Aboriginal women could meet with each other. There were some other charges directed at the organisers from Aboriginal women. So rather than create harmony the Fair created disunity. You know, I think it goes to show that there's a deeply entrenched psychological problem with racism for the majority of white women in this country. They really need to think about it and to address that. I don't believe it's for Aboriginal women to be the maids all the time or to be the helpers assisting white women to overcome their hang-ups, their guilt and their prejudices against Aboriginal people. It's for white women to do that. No matter what our best intentions are, perhaps we will never come together; I see that as a positive thing as much as I see it as a negative.

I certainly know the women I can trust and who I can work with and I cut out those that don't allow me and other Aboriginal women space to operate in. All I can do is make suggestions to non-Aboriginal women, to those feminists who I believe had a real concern about Indigenous women but don't quite know what to do about it. I would hope that by the year 2000 we would have some answers, but I'm not really confident yet. We might have progress in some directions, but there's been a legacy of over 200 years of deplorable treatment of Indigenous people by all non-Indigenous people, particularly the British colonisers who came to our country. We need to keep thinking all these issues through and see how we can deal with them.

Aunty Rita's File

When researching my Mother's life, the only available documents were housed in a Queensland government department. The process of obtaining information from the files was a long and arduous task. I thought it would be so simple – just ask for a file and it would appear. I was totally unaware of what might happen initially, and thankfully I went by myself to arrange the viewing. In 1996 I described the situation as well as my feelings.

——

Black people must redefine themselves and only they can do it. Throughout this country ... black communities are beginning to recognise the need to reassert their own definitions, to reclaim their history, their culture; to create their own sense of community and togetherness.

Stokely Carmichael

To attempt the reclamation of the history of our people that Stokely Carmichael urged is to encounter many folds of silence. Each fold is of the same cloth woven over two centuries of colonisation. There are, of course, the acts of violence, as well as massacre, that sought to silence us by alienating us from our own cultures and histories: the removal of people from their lands, the separation of children from their parents, the insistence on the surrender of our languages and customs, and the insistence on our adoption of European ways – the list goes on and continues into the present. These acts have been successful, to varying degrees, but people are beginning to tell such stories. There is still, however, that silence that you meet in Black Elders who cannot bear to speak of the humiliations and mutilations they have witnessed and experienced. But being silent has not been the way of my Mother, Aunty Rita.

When she and I decided, in 1990, that the time had come for us to write her story down, we sought access to my Mother's personal files which were held by the Department of Family Services and Aboriginal and Islander Affairs. I came to understand that the resistance that Aboriginal people meet in white bureaucrats when attempting to see Aboriginal records is one of the most contemporary forms that silencing takes.

Such files were compiled and kept on every person who had ever lived on a reserve; as it turned out, they were often continued long after that person had moved on. When I, as a historian, first made enquiries about seeing my Mother's files, I was made to watch across a huge desk as two white public servants turned the pages for me, one by one. Watch, don't touch – that was the rule. As I tried to read, the older man and his 18-year-old assistant would stop at particular pages themselves, at their pace, and read my Mother's file and whisper comments to each other that I could not hear.

These gatekeepers behaved as if the files were theirs, their property. They are not. They are my Mother's and my people's. These are my people's inheritance. At the same time as I was being made to sit through this, a white friend of ours, who was doing his PhD on the Cherbourg Reserve, was being given far greater access to these files than we would ever have been given. He was received as a credentialed researcher, whereas I was dismissed, I suppose, as just another Blackfellow wanting to know about her family's roots. But I didn't stop there, any more than my Mother did in her time.

It is important that the *Aboriginal* story of those times is told, otherwise it leaves our history to be whitewashed yet again. The 1950s were inhumane times for us (as every year has been since colonisation). But through all this destruction an identity and power did evolve, both individually and community-wide. Aboriginal people were pushed to the peripheries of white society. Still are. We are still shunned and excluded. But our treatment has also historically helped us – as city-Blacks, in the case of my Mother and me – to develop a greater capacity to negotiate on our terms. The story of my Mother's political resistance has to be told, as well as the story of her suffering.

The files I'm talking about are still retained by the Department but access by Aboriginal individuals and community groups has become less rigid. One may view the files of any individual, once permission has been granted by the eldest person in the family. (There could be problems with that criterion.) It has always been the case, since Freedom of Information legislation, that one may apply to view government files, but apparently access to the Department's files has taken longer to achieve. Well, these files are just like skeletal remains. We demand the return of our histories. And we demand a safe-keeping place for our files, one which Aboriginal people can trust, not one imposed on us, as white structures have always been. Until this happens, the whites continue to dominate our lives.

Later, when I returned to the Department with my Mother, to view the files together, I was quite sure that fresh scissor marks had appeared since my last visit. When I left that day, I felt anxious about the files' safety. I'd done my best, I'd swallowed my pride, I'd put up with the humiliation, but I'd caused the gatekeepers some alarm; you could see that in their behaviour towards us. And the local Murries were talking. The word was that whenever any interest had been expressed in any file, widespread shredding had begun.

Soon after, some Aboriginal friends started to work in the Department. One particular friend had actually been appointed supervisor over the two white bureaucrats, but even so, when she led us, my Mother and me, into an office where we could study Aunty Rita's files, she did so secretively, shutting the doors as we sat down, like we were criminals with no rights.

We were forewarned that the files could contain hurtful material. We were warned to remember the times when they were written and to keep in mind the paternalistic nature of those who did the writing. But nothing could have prepared my Mother for the experience of reading them.

The first entry was 1942 and the last was dated in 1974 – thirty-two years of surveillance. Whether my Mother's activism around Aboriginal issues had prolonged this policing is hard to tell, but common knowledge has it that most, if not all, ex-inmates of reserves had files kept on them in this way, whether they were politically active or not. It was enough that they were Aboriginal, that's all.

My Mother's file tells of many things. It tells, for instance, of outstanding bills from Myers. It features one rent bill for $30. 'Anyone would think I was a murderer,' my Mother said, 'but I guess there has to be something to keep those dorry public servants in a job. This just talks about the bad things in my life ... none of the positive, and there were many.'

It tells of the time that she ran away from the mission. We came to this part and my Mother looked up at me. She caught my eye. 'There are even comments here about my children. And you weren't born on the mission. You were born free.'

And so, together, we began the telling of Aunty Rita's life.

Queensland: Is the Clock Still Back 100 Years?

1997 was the 100th anniversary of the notorious Aboriginals Protection and the Restriction of the Sale of Opium Act of 1897. *FAIRA held a conference to ascertain the damage racism was doing to our society. On reflection, this article (written in 1997) was put together to depict the 'hooks' of important events which have contributed to the good and bad outcomes experienced by Indigenous peoples.*

—

Has anything changed in the last hundred years?

As a Murri I'm an eternal optimist; at the same time I'm an eternal pessimist, because I think once we feel things are going pretty well, along comes another insult to chop us down again. In this essay I will give you an overview of some events that have taken place over the past hundred years in terms of Indigenous affairs, and look at those events to see how they have changed the situation of Murries today.

So first, 1997 was the centenary of 'the Act', as it was commonly known – the Queensland Act that Aboriginal people had to endure. Certainly the grandmothers and grandfathers and parents of most Murri people reading this book, particularly those who lived in Brisbane, have come through that whole regime. The *Aborigines*

Protection and the Restriction of the Sale of Opium Act 1897, to give it its full title, provided the basis for a rigorous means of controlling and subjugating the Indigenous populations around Australia.

A major provision of the Act was the power to move Aborigines forcibly to and from areas designated as reserves by the State. The removal program had a devastating impact on Aboriginal communities and lifestyles. People were taken from their country; wives were separated from husbands; children taken from parents; and the elderly isolated from their children and grandchildren.

These processes separated not only Blacks from whites, but also tore apart generations from each other's keeping, as well as in many instances separating males from females. I argue that we Aboriginal people are all products of the Stolen Generations, whether we were taken directly from our parents or not. Being shunted around and incarcerated on Aboriginal missions and reserves meant that people were stolen from their country, which in many ways is just as devastating as having been stolen from your parents, because of our special relationship to the land.

In May 1902 Minnie Koran, a resident of Rockhampton in central Queensland, was taken from her home by police and held overnight in the watchhouse. Minnie's husband protested to the local magistrate but to no avail. The following day she was put on a train and sent to Brisbane, accompanied by the notorious Archibald Meston, the southern Protector of Aborigines at the time. Although charged with no offence, Minnie Koran's crime was that she was an Aboriginal woman. Archibald Meston, acting on his powers under the Act, ordered her removal to a reserve, for her own 'good and protection'. Yet as Minnie was to discover when she arrived at the Durandur Reserve in southern Queensland, Mr Meston had ordered her removal so that she could be forcibly married to a Black man at the mission. She wrote in anguish to her actual husband, 'I won't get married to nobody as I am already married to you.'

One hundred years later we are free to move around our country and live where we wish – provided the landlord says it's okay to have Blacks there. This was something I had to go through recently because I was moving house and looking for a house to rent. I was in awe, I guess, of having to see real estate agents and checking out the rental market again. It doesn't matter how educated you are, how you speak, how you dress, what car you drive, what house you live in, or what suburb you live in, by nature of being visibly Aboriginal you are an instant target.

As I was house hunting, I thought that, provided I can get past the barriers of discrimination that still exist in pursuing a rental property and the landlord says it's okay, I might be able to live where I want. Of course, we now have the freedom to marry whom we want to and, in fact, not to marry. So those freedoms obviously exist. However, racial stereotypes are still applied to us as Aboriginal people. The colonial mentality has, in the past twelve to eighteen months, had a resurgence particularly in Queensland, and we see all the old colonial attitudes that were once around being dished out to us again.

When I was recently in London I gave a paper on Captain Cook and his voyages to the southern oceans. Although the situation has changed in many ways since Cook's time, the manner in which we are still viewed by the international and wider community, generally speaking, is as though we are descended from the apes. Certainly that is the stereotype which I found still held in countries like England, Germany and France.

I'd like now to write about a few important dates and what they mean for Indigenous people. We can see that there is a whole range of successful things that have happened, I believe, because of the resistance of Indigenous people rather than the goodwill of government. Of course there has been some goodwill in the Australian community – a better goodwill in the past than that which exists today – which acknowledges our efforts and our struggles to be recognised.

Going back to 1852, we had the European and the Chinese rush to the goldfields. In 1875 the Palmer River goldfield opened up and Aboriginal resistance to Europeans and Chinese was defeated. I think this is very interesting, because many of us Murries are descended from Asian people. Some people say that we, the Aboriginal people, came from Asia.

I was told in London that during the Ice Age, you know how all the land mass was joined up, we came from Tibet. I wonder how you respond to people who make these comments when they don't have any knowledge about Dreaming and Dreamtime and spirituality. There are two views in this country about how the Indigenous people came to be here. One is a scientific theory of migration, and the other is a true belief in Dreamtime and spirituality, and that as Indigenous people we evolved from the land.

The Aboriginal people's experience with the immigration of Asians and Europeans has had a long history, and I almost think the ghosts are coming to revisit us as we fend off racism. In the 1850s European immigration extended to the New South Wales frontier, west, and north into Queensland. By the 1860s, white settlement had extended into the Northern Territory and to far north Queensland. From that decade on, the protection policies relating to Aboriginal people were instituted by the Australian Government. Almost a century later, in 1940, the assimilation policy was announced. As we know, assimilation policies have never worked for Aboriginal and Torres Strait Islander people, nor should they. We should be able to retain our dignity and self-respect as the First Nation people of this country without assimilating with anybody, being expected to regard ourselves as white, and holding white values.

By the 1960s the benefit of the assimilation policies for Aborigines began to be questioned. However, many people say to me in the current climate, 'Well, you know, shouldn't you assimilate?' and I categorically say 'no' to them, because assimilation is an act of genocide, far worse than any protection policies, far worse.

On 6 February 1939 the first strike was organised by Aboriginal people. It was in response to the brutality of officials at Cummeragunja mission in New South Wales who treated the Aboriginal people like animals. They were driven to open revolt by this treatment – 300 Aborigines walked off the station and marched into Victoria two weeks later. Also 1939, and continuing to 1945, saw the participation of Aboriginal servicemen and women in World War II. There were the Aboriginal freedom rides in 1963, when Charlie Perkins accompanied by Sydney University students travelled to north and north-western New South Wales to draw attention to the social discrimination, housing conditions and employment problems of Aboriginal people.

In May 1966 the Aboriginal pastoral workers employed by the Vesteys Corporation in the Northern Territory went out on strike for equal pay with whites, which they received after a very protracted battle. In 1966 the Equal Pay Claim of Cattlemen brought attention to the wage inequalities in the pastoral industry.

On 27 May 1967 we witnessed the Referendum which gave us citizenship rights. Some people still believe that it gave us the right to vote. Well, it didn't. There were obscure mechanisms in place way before that which gave Aboriginal people voting rights, but they were very restricted – for example you had to own property or serve in the First or Second World Wars (you had to have one white parent in order to serve in those wars anyhow). Aboriginal people in the 1960s and the decades before were not given a reasonable education. Many were not even taught to speak English, so they could not know their rights as voting people within Australian society.

The 1970s saw the legal aid services introduced. Also at this time, as many Murries will remember, Aboriginal people began to form a number of visible community organisations in Brisbane. Further down the track, in the late 1970s to the early 1980s, I was very proud to be part of the process which established some of these organisations.

In January 1972 an Aboriginal Tent Embassy was set up on the lawns of Parliament House, Canberra. Hundreds of Aborigines occupied the Embassy in shifts, day and night, for six months. It was a famous focus for Aboriginal demands for justice. The police tore down the tents on instructions from the government after violent clashes with hundreds of Aborigines and their white supporters. One week later the Tent Embassy was re-established, and again torn down. A law was passed forbidding camping in a public place in Canberra, but the tents went up again, which shows the true resistance of Aboriginal people.

Who can forget that on 26 January 1988 Aboriginal people declared a day of mourning for the 200th anniversary of the invasion of our country? A festival was held to commemorate the 200th birthday party of Australia, but for the Aboriginal people it marked 200 years of misery and degradation imposed on our ancestors by the white invaders of this country.

Now the blame for the misery in which so many Aboriginal people live has been placed on us and many of our services are being severely eroded or taken away.

So have things changed in the last hundred years? In structural ways they have changed, and some of these are good changes. All of these, though, have been at the initiative of Aboriginal and Torres Strait Islander people. There has been an effort from governments to provide funding and to service these changes. However, why do we still find ourselves with the worst unemployment, the worst housing, the most poorly educated people, the worst in terms of our health? There is something severely wrong here. While many things have improved, many things have not really changed. In fact, they've regressed.

I do see, however, that there is a future for all of us: a future for our children, our grandchildren, and for each other. I would not be doing the type of work that I do unless I knew that one was possible.

We can all dwell a little on the past, and I think this is necessary, but we also need to get on with the future and think about how it can be better for our children and other children who are coming up – and for each other as Indigenous and non-Indigenous people in this country.

Bringing Them Home

Besides being a mother, the hardest 'other' job I've performed is that of Queensland Co-Commissioner for the Inquiry into the Separation of Aboriginal and Torres Strait Islander Children from Their Families. Many people asked what it was like and my usual reply was that it was like being put through a wringer and pulled out slowly so that all the tears could dry. The 'Bringing Them Home' report had a significant impact on the wider Australian community, far more than those of us involved in the Inquiry could have imagined. I wrote this piece in 1998.

——

A constructive response from the government to the 'Bringing Them Home' report of the national Inquiry into the Separation of Aboriginal and Torres Strait Islander Children from Their Families is vital to the process of reconciliation.

The cruel policy of separating children from their families has left behind legacies of grief for its victims and destruction of cultural identity.

I believe I was approached to become a Co-Commissioner for the Inquiry because of my knowledge of the past policies, practices and legislation gained as a historian of Aboriginal issues. But this knowledge came not only from textbooks; it is very real to me because I experienced many of the repressive policies and practices as I was growing up. My Mother was under the 1897 Preservation and Protection Act, I grew up in the assimilation era, and when I started work it was called the self-determination era. I've been under and in so many Acts now that I've joined a cast of thousands queuing up for Actor's Equity. Then, Indigenous people are natural-born actors; we act up for the courts, police, judges, bosses. We've been acting all our lives.

Sometimes I think I've got one of those faces that says 'Pick me, pick me!' The Inquiry transformed me in ways which meant I could never be the same person again. It made me realise how little I knew about history.

Like many people, I grew up with my family and never questioned the absurdity of anyone ever taking me away. I felt safe, controlled, loved, wanted and encouraged. Any child who starts off with this premise can only hope for a better future. My wonderful Mother always said to give your children the best possible start in life and it will stay with them forever. This affirmation is essential for everyone but even more for an Aboriginal child, as there is an extra dimension and responsibility of imbuing a deep sense of pride in being born Aboriginal.

This is where the chain has been broken for many of the Stolen-Generation children. They could not receive the teachings from their peers and family once they were ripped away. Their culture and identity have been fractured. They are told they are too Black to be white and too white to be Black. So where do they fit? Many times they have to go back and relearn the whole Aboriginal community politics, dynamics, how to behave, the protocols, as well as try to link up with their mob. There are huge pressures for these people. The psychological problems this presents relegates our people into further institutions.

When I wrote a perspectives article for Brisbane's *Courier-Mail* about saying sorry to the children, I received some hate mail for the first time in my life. Now how on earth anyone would want to deny a child its rightful place to be with its mother, father and family is totally beyond my comprehension. I disposed of the letters with my junk mail. But I am aware that there are those who see any gains by Indigenous peoples as threats.

The stories of the Stolen Generation must be told. All Australians need to understand this episode in our history, not as an abstract piece of knowledge, but as the cause of so much pain and hurt borne by Indigenous peoples today. The 'Bringing Them Home' report challenges the nation's capacity to face the truth of its part in it and to deal with it in an open and compassionate way. It is only when the realities are faced that the nation will be able to come up with the remedies.

We cannot look at the Stolen Generation report as a catalogue of isolated incidents which happened in the dim, dark ages – back in our grandmothers' and grandfathers' time. The people I interviewed for the Inquiry were in their 20s and 30s, so it's not that long ago really.

These people told of the abuse they had suffered, many times how they were told that they had no family, only to find them many years later, and sometimes too late. The saddest stories I heard were from people who had finally tracked down their mother or father only to find they had died a few weeks earlier.

Imagine that, not ever knowing your parents, your brothers and sisters. It's incomprehensible to those of us who have always had them. We treasure them, argue with them. They are always there for us. Having no family to turn to is a horrendous twist of fate.

So the best advice I can give to people who are trying to understand this process is to put yourself in their shoes. Think what it would have been like if one day someone dragged you away and put you in an Aboriginal family where you never saw your real parents and family again. You grew up Aboriginal, danced, sang and ate witchetty grubs. Which for some of us would be a blessing, so maybe I should use another oppositional culture ... but I can't think of one!

I have heard people say 'but it happened to white people too', and while we can never deny their suffering as well, they were not taken away on the basis of their race. In operation at the time was the assimilation policy which basically and cruelly meant that Aboriginal people would be forced to deny their culture and heritage, be imbued with white values, attitudes and behaviours. One lady on the radio recently said to me that she looked after a boy as a 'white Blackfella'. He had had a note on his file stamped 'never to be returned'. I presumed this meant 'never to be returned' to his family because of his Aboriginality.

These stories must be told because for far too long the silence has been festering like an unhealed wound. Here in Queensland we have suggested to some Church educational bodies and the State Education Department that students should become aware of the report, its history and its implications. Students will then gain a greater appreciation of the circumstances and history of the Stolen Generation.

The 'Bringing Them Home' report was tabled in Parliament during the Australian Reconciliation Convention on 26 May 1997. This date has now been designated as a National Sorry Day. At the convention participants were given an opportunity to turn to their Indigenous neighbours and apologise for the past hurts that they had suffered. On the inaugural Sorry Day, 7 February 1998, 5000 non-Indigenous people in King George Square in Brisbane were given that opportunity by the Lord Mayor, Jim Soorley.

The Reconciliation Convention subsequently called on all parliaments, local governments, organisations and institutions to follow this example and to offer their own apology, 'so that we can all move forward together to share responsibility for the future of this nation'.

There has been a huge groundswell of parliaments, organisations and individuals apologising and asking for justice for the survivors. Most state and territory governments, churches and schools, professional associations and local government authorities have expressed their particular apologies. A Sorry Book of signatures and comments were organised on local and national levels.

While the Prime Minister's personal apology at the Convention and the Senate's subsequent apology were welcome, it is a shame that the Government on behalf of the nation is not prepared to offer a similar apology. I have thought recently about the absence of this apology and have wondered if a shallow apology would be good enough.

But the recommendations of the Convention cannot wait for a federal apology. There are many that can be implemented at the local and state level without a great outlay of resources. Schools, churches and community groups can assist. I chair a Steering Group of a coalition of stakeholders that are interested in the report's implementation at the Queensland state level. We have responses already of what can be done. Some of the hurts can be alleviated, such as by dealing with records, educating parishioners, putting Aboriginal history into curriculums, setting up reunions, and by counselling and education sessions.

For some months the Brisbane City Council, the Indigenous community and Queensland Churches worked together to organise various ceremonies in Brisbane to acknowledge the wrongful removal of children.

And as I wrote this, the tears flowed just remembering that incredible Saturday evening on 7 February [1998] when Murries gathered in Musgrave Park for a symbolic march into the city at dusk. The air was filled with emotion because now we were reclaiming our right to enter the city limits. In the past there was an ordinance to keep our people out of the city and confined to South Brisbane and West End and northern areas. 'Boundary Streets' in various suburbs mark the boundaries of the city beyond which Aboriginal people could not pass. They were not allowed to enter the city area.

In Musgrave, prior to the march, we welcomed back to our Indigenous community our Black brothers and sisters who had been stolen. And then at dusk a large group of Murries marched into King George Square where thousands of non-Aboriginal people welcomed us back to the city and home. Someone said to me, 'You know, I saw all those whitefellas standing up there clapping – and I turned around. No one else was there, they were clapping for us – I couldn't believe it! You know, Sis, we're not alone, are we?'

Unlike the colonial days, now we have a viable people's movement of those willing to stand up and be counted with us. The voices are speaking out loud and strong and the actions are speaking even louder than the words. The healing has begun.

Those of us involved in the Inquiry asked that the report be received with an open heart and mind. Under the leadership of Brisbane Lord Mayor Jim Soorley and with the participants, that Saturday was more than we could have ever hoped and wished for. The national spotlight was on Brisbane and the success of the event will now be measured across the nation.

This is what you can do for the Stolen Generation:

- Forgiveness and healing requires coming to terms with this painful episode in Australian history, through learning about the truth and understanding the consequences. In other words, read, view and become educated yourselves. Don't think it's all too hard or complex because it's quite simple really. If you walk away from it, you walk away from the truth and the opportunity to become informed.
- Provide venues where people who feel comfortable about telling their stories are permitted to do so. Remember it is not only about their healing but ours too, together.

- Sincerely, sincerely apologise and participate in the National Sorry Day. If you have never been involved in one activity in your life this is it. Just your presence and participation is an act of compassion.
- The issue of reparation, or restitution, to the survivors must be addressed not just as part of the process towards justice, but as part of the national healing process.

If these things are done it will bring about the long-awaited justice and healing that needs to progress. The stuff that we felt last Saturday night – a pure cleansing. Only once we do this can we walk together.

The Gift of Identity

All my life I have wanted to explain what identity has meant to me, with a view to others exploring theirs. To be honest I get annoyed about opportunistic identifiers on the Aboriginal scene, of which I have seen many when others have had to suffer the indignities of what our race would bring for the rest of our lives. For whatever reason they chose not to identify is their business and I don't buy into it these days. Mother said to me when I became a mother, 'Make sure you give that boy his identity and culture. Make sure he knows he belongs and where he comes from.' Luckily that's what I did and it worked. As this essay, which was first published in ATSIC News *in February 2001, explains, identity is indeed a gift.*

———

The terms of identity/Aboriginality/Indigeneity may have many definitions among Indigenous Australians. Due to diversity throughout Australia a range of definitions about identity may be possible. Identity is private and public or, in other words, both personal and political. Aboriginality cannot be expressed in words as it is a feeling of one's own spirituality. At best, it can be described to non-Aboriginals as a sense of deep, proud cultural identity. Aboriginals live it and express it every day through art, language, humour, beliefs and familial and community relationships. Aboriginality forms the core basis of identity.

While there have been attempts to address aspects of identity, these have been derived mainly from early Europeans, government officials, anthropologists, historians and other researchers who have attempted to define identity to suit their preconceived ideas. There are infinite numbers of examples among them. In order to provide jurisdiction over Aboriginals, a part of the Queensland 1939 Aborigines Act stated that an Aborigine was 'Any half-blood who lives as wife or husband with an Aboriginal, or who habitually associates with Aboriginals.'

Various government policies have attempted to erode Aboriginality. The Northern Territory Aboriginal Ordinance of 1911 authorised the removal of mixed-race children from their parents to an institution. Separations of this nature had drastic consequences for identities of these children. Aboriginal values were replaced by European values, which created alienation of Aboriginal children from the culture of their parents. The child was torn between two cultures and could not relate to either Aboriginal or European society. The Stolen Generation story is all too familiar and a part of our history.

Identity is formed by social processes. It is this identity that has built Indigenous ideology for living and survival. Once understood it is maintained, adapted and remodelled depending on challenges and circumstance. Although the colonisation and urbanisation process has attempted to impose its alien value system on Indigenous peoples in order to immobilise traditional lifestyles and values, the concept of identity or Aboriginality has enabled Aboriginals to cope with the traumatic experiences of city living.

In urban environments the ever-increasing mobility and advanced technology inevitably change people's values and culture. Urbanisation may break down many cultural ties and limit traditional practices and beliefs, thus changing people's concepts of their way of life. Consequently, demands have been imposed on Indigenous people living in cities to undergo drastic cultural changes. It is in many ways a tough outside world and the maintenance of Aboriginality provides a security against this but should not be viewed as romanticism.

While various social scientists have explored concepts of identity both hideous and romantic, most commentators have failed to perceive the insider's view – how Black people themselves perceive and understand their conditions. In the study of urban Aboriginal cultures, this emphasis must be reversed, to concentrate on the internal social structure rather than the external social structure.

One such internal structure is the system of kinship, which determines behaviour and the responsibility of every individual within the society towards every other person. This social organisation is a principle in Aboriginal traditional society and has in effect survived and carried over to urban society although not as intricately. Urbanisation endeavours to force people to become individuals rather than members of a particular family, clan or kinship group.

Fundamental to the principle of identity is land. The fight of Indigenous people today for their lands and waters is a struggle for the right to maintain their identity. In an ideal world, legally secured native title rights, a secure base, sovereignty and the rights to self-determination are enhanced. Without identity deculturation is guaranteed along with dispossession and dispersal. Without sovereignty, deprivation and dependency are legacies facing Indigenous peoples. This has been the continuing wound between Indigenous and non-Indigenous Australians. The talk of treaty has again been opened up on the political landscape. It remains to be seen what the content, consultation, and negotiation processes will offer identity issues.

An often overlooked but remarkable characteristic of identity and survival is humour. Humour is an integral and warm concept of Indigenous societies. The experiences, perspectives and needs of many Aboriginal people are so diverged from the majority of white Australians that the reality from a Black perspective is not readily understood. Aboriginals draw humour from situations and definitions about them that would prove painful and offensive if told by others. A substantial amount of Aboriginal humour if revealed to outsiders would not have struck them as funny. Humour allows for the liberating of feelings that normally are contained. The liberation brings relief and pleasure, which helps to explain why humour has been notably present among people who seem to outsiders to have little to laugh about. Humour has also allowed Black people to laugh thereby gaining some perspective on their own anger.

The essence of identity is complex and multilayered. Although many attempts have been made to assimilate Aboriginal people into wider Australian society they have never succeeded. This has been largely due to the resilience, kinship, family and community orientation of Indigenous society. Other factors such as land, language, humour and identity have also influenced the transmission of Aboriginality and this has persisted to the present and will continue to provide future generations with strength, dignity and purpose. The greatest gift any Indigenous parent can give to their child is the gift of identity. All else follows.

Indigenous Women and Leadership: A Personal Reflection

In 2004 I was privileged to join my two leadership mentors, Kerrie Tim and Anne Dunn, in delivering commonwealth government Women's Leadership programs across the country. In writing this piece for an internal handbook, it helped me crystalise my experience, thoughts and aspirations to pass on to the very willing participants. To this day I encounter these women who are now leaders in their own communities, boldly out front and centre. It makes me incredibly proud of their achievements and they acknowledge how this program sent them on their journeys. The confidence building and embracing each other in where they were at and where and who they wanted to be was inspiring and, of course, one of the best jobs I have ever had.

—

It's impossible to write about being Indigenous, being a woman and the challenges of leadership without reflecting on my own feelings and experiences, the things that guide and inspire me, and the tough aspects of playing all these roles at the same time.

To my mind, you cannot speak about the need for leadership within our communities without being prepared to take on responsibility yourself. It's not enough to point the finger at those who have let us down and to expect others to come forward and fix our problems.

Nor can anyone afford to call themselves a leader unless they truly have the interests of our community at heart. Too many people like to think they are leaders and too many are identified by the media as leaders who are not really leaders at all.

The reality of being a leader is not necessarily about earning big money or being recognised on the street. And this is particularly true of our women leaders, many of whom work tirelessly, thanklessly, behind the scenes to make their communities healthy.

Women leaders face great sacrifices, especially in terms of the time they would prefer to spend with family, let alone having time to themselves for rest and recreation. For single mothers, like me, there is a heavy toll and were it not for family support mechanisms, these extra responsibilities would be impossible to fulfil.

So what are the challenges of leadership for Indigenous women?

Number one, it's about putting yourself 'out there' in the first place. People in our communities are very suspicious of those who stand out from the crowd or big note themselves. There is a real danger that you can be seen as a tall poppy, and there is much jealousy and envy in our community.

It's important to strike a balance, and there's a fine line between achieving that balance and putting people offside.

The essential rule to follow as a leader is to never forget where you've come from or who put you there. Stay in touch with your local mob, especially the Aunties and Uncles. I have Aunties back home who pray for me all the time in the work that I do, and they tell me this whenever they see me. It is an enormous comfort to me.

The greatest challenge out there in the wider community, I believe, is that non-Indigenous people judge you by different standards. You get by if you present well and are articulate, and if you are consistent with your messages. A good education goes a long way – I have been blessed by it and am very proud to have it.

All leaders are actors in the different roles they play and in the wider community you are expected to be able to modify your behaviour and language in different situations without losing sight of who you are.

The ability to communicate with people from all walks of life is important. My son often says I am a chameleon, changing my communication styles depending on whom I'm talking to. It's true in many ways but it's not a bad thing – I enjoy the challenge of good communication and using it to bring out the best in people.

My family keeps me grounded so that none of this goes to my head or changes me at the core. Without family and the support I receive from women generally, plus the people I work with, Indigenous and non-Indigenous, it would be a lot harder to do what I do. I draw on them for comfort, support and nourishment all the time. You simply cannot do this stuff on your own or without accepting help from others.

The other thing I would say about leadership is that people can pick phonies (especially my mob). If you are not fair dinkum, if you put on airs and graces and are not being yourself, you're finished.

Be natural and with a bit of spit and polish from your minders, if you are lucky enough to have them, it will happen for you.

Respect other people as much as you respect yourself. Be confident in who you are and what you can produce. As a leader, you should never say things that you don't mean or that you wouldn't want others to overhear. If you don't know the answer to a question, be honest about it because people respect and respond to that honesty. My message comes from my gut reaction sometimes and I find this to be the most powerful instinct of all.

Take an interest in everybody, no matter how significant or insignificant they are, or think they are. We are all part of this evolving human race.

The responsibilities of leadership for women in our communities are all-encompassing, incorporating everything from dealing with domestic violence to sending the children to school. Just identifying the extent of these responsibilities is exhausting.

They are different for each community and situation, as we are not homogenous. Leadership means that you need to respect differences of views and start from where people are at – not where you want them to be. The trick is to listen, listen, listen, and then act. Manage your often-competing responsibilities by using your networks. Never promise to do something that you cannot do. Never let people down – if you can't help them, let them know and they will respect you for it. Be personable but truthful – leadership that is not reliable will inevitably come back to bite you.

It is an inspiration that, increasingly, Aboriginal women have our own models of leadership demonstrated, such as through women like Evelyn Scott and Lowitja O'Donoghue. For me there was also Doris Pilkington and May O'Brien. These senior Indigenous women showed true strength. I look up to them and many others, and learn from them according to our Indigenous way of learning and acquiring knowledge.

Often I sought their counsel and advice on issues. The strength and dignity of having gone through a lifetime of trauma and survived to become true leaders is something that we should all aspire to as Indigenous women.

Finally, I must come to the core challenges faced by Indigenous women leaders: racism and sexism. And again, I can only really comment on these challenges by reflecting on how they have affected me.

First of all, I identify as a human being. Then Aboriginal. Then woman, Mother, Sister, Aunt. And then to my professional roles at Reconciliation Australia and The University of Queensland.

Indigenous women experience simultaneous oppressions including sexism and racism, and sometimes it's hard to pinpoint which oppression is being experienced at a particular time. If you are dark-skinned and look Aboriginal, most often it's racism.

When I look in the mirror each morning, I see a Black face. As I look a bit longer, I see the face of a woman. My first identity is that of my race. So with all the trials and tribulations of being a female Aboriginal leader, that is what I feel I face up to first. Accordingly, my deepest connection and priority is to Indigenous people.

Sexism was more of an issue for me when I was much younger, and I know this is still the case for young Indigenous women I work alongside. Sexism gets easier as you get older and grow in senior woman status. Perhaps the men become more respectful and a little more frightened of you!

But it was always racism that I felt as a much greater liability for me in achieving what I wanted to achieve. What I would say is that women who experience sexism or racism must confront these forms of discrimination head on and never tolerate or accept them.

In addressing all the difficult sides of leadership – and they are very real – I should also reflect on the wonderful aspects of being identified as someone who cares for their community. That is why it is so important for women to make themselves known in different capacities within their own communities. If your community doesn't know who you are, leadership is much harder, much less legitimate.

I had the great advantage of coming from a well-known and respected family that was always part of the community. Once your community sees you doing things for it, people feel and show pride and support, which is the greatest of gifts and reinforcements. It far outweighs the difficulties of leadership.

And when you are noticed for the good job you are doing in the community, there's a chain reaction where you are identified to take on bigger and broader responsibilities. This is why there is such a hunger for emerging young Indigenous leaders at the national level and why it's vital for older leaders to mentor, communicate and allow younger people to take the lead also.

It's a very Aboriginal thing to do, to give younger people greater responsibilities within the community as they become able to take on those responsibilities. It is a culturally appropriate transfer of roles that involves respect in both directions – from the younger to the older and the older to the younger.

Every day I speak to my Mother who passed on eight years ago. Every day I ask her to guide me in my journeys. When I have to speak at a big event, when I am restless and nervous, I meditate for a few moments and I feel her tap on my shoulder to tell me she is there with me.

She then calls in the ancestors and I am surrounded by them. They tell me to 'go for it'. Which is what I have done – and tell my young Sisters to do also.

The 1967 Referendum ... Four Decades Later

This was a farewell speech I gave in 2007 after my time on both the Council for Aboriginal Reconciliation and Reconciliation Australia coincided with the 40th anniversary of the momentous 1967 Referendum. In my time with these organisations from 1995–2007 I was fortunate to have the services of a fine speech-writer, Claire Tedeschi, who I said always made me look good. We had worked out a position where she would know my rhythm and voice and what I wanted to say. To get the best from me she would probe, ask questions and then weave her magic. There were so many speeches I performed while in the public space. It became effortless every time I had a gig to do.

—

I would like to acknowledge the Traditional Owners of the land on which we are meeting, the Gadigal people, who are one of twenty-nine clan groups in the Sydney Metropolitan area referred to collectively as the Eora Nation. I pay my respects to Elders past and present, and to all Aboriginal people within these boundaries.

Thank you, Gerard Henderson, Head of Sydney Institute, for the opportunity to speak here this evening, during a week that means more to me than I'm able to convey. In some ways I feel my life has been building up to this for forty years – the choices I've made and even the person I've become. And it all culminates this Sunday when, together with fellow directors from Reconciliation Australia, I will be honoured in hosting for a few days in Canberra survivors from the campaign that led to the 1967 Referendum – the most successful in our nation's history by a mile.

We've had acceptances from thirty-five of the original campaigners, many of them now elderly and frail. We've been talking with them about the anniversary over eight or nine months, learning more about their stories, and hearing new stories of people they campaigned alongside. And they have all said the same thing about how the 40th anniversary of this most unusually successful referendum should be approached.

But let me come back to this week's commemorations in a few minutes. Because the opportunity Gerard offered me to speak about the anniversary has had me thinking a great deal about my own life, conducting a kind of internal retrospective. I hope you'll bear with me as I share some of my thoughts and memories with you.

I remember the day of the 1967 Referendum well and see it still, in many ways, through the eyes of the 11-year-old girl I was at the time. And I also remember some of the long lead-up to it. If I was asked to make one more toffee or lamington for a fundraising drive (or do the hula) or stand on another street corner handing out badges ...

My Father died when I was two and I was raised by a determined Mother who was politically involved in the early years. The Referendum campaign became my dear Mother's life, and it shaped mine. Those social functions and fundraisers were an opportunity to knock on the doors of people who'd never met an Aboriginal person before and to let them know we were still here after so many different attempts to silence us.

We children didn't quite fathom the significance of what happened on 27 May 1967. I do remember the shrieks of joy after the result was announced, laughter and a mass of tears. Mum told me we would be counted in the census now, along with the sheep and cattle. She also said we would be free people at last. I never quite knew what she meant, only that this was a big deal.

It's a time that also gave me my earliest memories of the struggle that Aboriginal and non-Aboriginal people have fought together, recognising that if a group of us is not free in this country, nor are the rest of us. It's the struggle that at some stage we started calling reconciliation. Lots of people hate the word, Black and white people, but it seems to be a word we're stuck with now. And people have to work out for themselves what it means and doesn't mean. I reckon it's also about your actions and what you do rather than a label.

As a child, I loved to communicate with people and never felt too shy. Mum would take me around on her culture talks and people would ask me questions. Sometimes it felt like a challenge to answer them but I've always tried and that gave me enormous satisfaction. Still does.

Like my Mother, I've always wanted to reach non-Aboriginal people as well as my own people and I suppose this explains, in part, why I was drawn, and keep being drawn, to reconciliation. I was schooled by the early reconciliationists in this country. I think I had reconciliation in my genes.

And, to me, like my Mother who understood what it meant a long time before the struggle was called anything, reconciliation has always encompassed three things: recognition, justice and healing.

Recognition that, as the First Peoples of this country, we have existed here over 70,000 years and are one of the oldest surviving cultures on the planet. That we have maintained and cared for land and for people.

Justice is about overcoming all the social disadvantages that can be summed up in one stunning statistic that says our children can expect to die on average seventeen years earlier than the children of other Australians. I have absolutely no doubt that we can only meet this enormous challenge of amending that if we work together as Indigenous and non-Indigenous people who care about it. That we work together with trust and with respect.

Healing, because that is really our fundamental goal as human beings, will only be achieved if in this country we achieve reconciliation. And it ain't gonna happen if the spiritual side of reconciliation gets neglected. You can have so-called practical reconciliation where you give a Blackfella a house, a car or a job, but if the symbolic is not addressed then we will never achieve reconciliation in this country. By the symbolic, I mean all the many things that have to do with building a respectful relationship.

The balance needs to be right.

Many good Australians have nurtured the flowers of this noble cause over the last forty years, people who understand how much better it would be for all of us to live together respectfully, and be able to share in this country's vast opportunity and prosperity.

It was something Australians understood in 1967, if only for a moment, but it has driven and inspired many people since, more and more people all the time. And not just a certain type of person – left leaning, religious, or just people who like stirring the pot. Lots of different kinds of Australians support reconciliation. They're people who understand when something's not fair and know that something should be done about it. People in business, in government, in media, all the different professions and political persuasions. People you meet in supermarkets.

The reason I think more and more people are getting involved in reconciliation lately, and I'm talking more about whitefellas at the moment, is that they're feeling not only should something be done about Indigenous disadvantage, but maybe something *can* be done about it. They're hearing enough good stuff happening involving Indigenous people to think things can be better. Enough to chip away at their misconceptions.

But getting there is going to require of us, Indigenous and non-Indigenous, that we shift out of entrenched positions. We need to see and learn about what's actually working in improving Indigenous people's lives, and think about how we can reasonably apply it in different contexts. We need to be prepared to listen to one another.

This week's Referendum anniversary is a good thing for Australians to hear about and think about because it marks a fine and decisive choice once made by the people of this nation. And the explanation as to why it happened is to be found much earlier than those final ten years where we find the stories that tell us more about the how.

The job may have to be finished in the Parliament and with a vice-regal signature but the real work is done in kitchens and workplace cafeterias, camps and community halls.

This didn't start like any other movement for constitutional change, just because a government wanted it to. It started because enough of the Australian people wanted it.

The stories of the 1967 Referendum go at least as far back as the 1870s, when Louisa Briggs stood up against conditions on the Coranderrk Aboriginal station in Victoria. She worked as a nurse there to support her nine children until she protested about starvation-level rations and demanded cash wages, and was removed from the reserve. The only way Louisa could keep her children was to move around. Because she didn't accept government policy like the word of God.

People who knew Louisa described her as audacious and strong-minded. Her place in Australian political history hasn't been recognised, but her story is one of the important ones on the road to a referendum that took place ninety years later. It's one of many worth retelling now that we are so much better equipped in so many ways to make good on the choice Australians made in 1967.

I also love the story of Hetty Perkins, an Arrendte woman who supported her family by working as a nursemaid in Alice Springs but changed jobs and started cooking and washing on the reserve so she could be near her children. Hetty Perkins didn't confront white authority, she avoided it, making sure her children had the benefit of learning around the campfires as well as at school. One of Hetty's children was Charles Perkins, the first Aboriginal head of a government department – set up as a result of the 1967 Referendum.

Pearl Gibbs' story takes us right up to the Referendum. She was from Brewarrina but grew up around Ngunawal people in Yass, at the same time politicians were deciding which bit of Ngunawal land to take as the site for a national capital. Pearl had three children, supporting them by working as a cook in the homes of Sydney's well-to-do. Well, Pearl cooked up more than the dinner in those kitchens.

When she found out that Aboriginal girls working as domestics were indentured to the Protection Board, she started a campaign that ended the practice. When she found that vegetables delivered to her kitchen door were picked by people who could never earn enough to buy them, she organised a strike by pea pickers on the Shoalhaven. Pearl drew big crowds in the Domain in the 1930s when she spoke for the Aborigines' Progressive Association. She was one of the organisers of the Day of Mourning on 26 January 1938 and belonged to every group in New South Wales that was campaigning for Aboriginal rights, white and Black.

There are so many wonderful stories that help explain what eventually happened in 1967. They show how people can't help but be attracted by courage for good. And the fact that I've mentioned three women here shouldn't suggest to you that there were not a whole lot of men working for reconciliation, Black and white.

Australians need to know about these networks of change-makers who brought out the best in us. Because the best is always there waiting to be tapped by true leaders in our communities.

Pearl Gibbs and Faith Bandler are recognised names, who were prominent players in the better known parts of the Referendum story. So was Jessie Street who worked with Faith in Sydney, complaining when she discovered Faith 'wasting her time' making curtains for a new home when she should have been circulating a draft petition.

There was Shirley Andrews and Brian Fitzpatrick in Melbourne, Oodgeroo Noonucal and Stan McBride in Brisbane, the Duguids and Don Dunstan in Adelaide. And less prominent, mighty campaigners like Herb Simms in Sydney and Mary Bennett in Kalgoorlie – it's a great cast of true leaders.

And for the names we know, there are many more we don't. And never will, because in 1967 there were just so many Australians who got involved.

Along with the Federal Council for the Advancement of Aborigines and Torres Strait Islanders (FCAATSI) at the national level there were state- and territory-based Aboriginal rights groups, such as OPAL in Brisbane and the Victorian Aboriginal Advancement League in Melbourne, who used their numbers to mobilise around the campaign. People who'd heard about the campaign in their churches or women's groups or trades unions. And they'd tell their families and their friends and workmates, who then told their neighbours. It was many, many conversations that joined in a spirit of reconciliation and became a national determination. The kind of determination I believe I'm sensing again in Australia.

I'm proud of how Reconciliation Australia is using this anniversary to commemorate past, great achievements but also to persuade and inspire and if necessary entertain people into understanding how much they should and can do now. I said a few minutes ago that the Referendum campaigners who are making their way to Canberra later this week all say the same thing about what they want from the anniversary. And it's not praise or publicity. They want to convey to young Australians that a lot can be achieved when you tap into the best in people. Frankly, they also want to give a whole lot of people a kick up the backside and tell them to get on with it.

Talking directly with people about hard issues and seeing them listen makes me feel we're getting somewhere. Seeing my students getting degrees and good jobs and making good lives for themselves are positive news stories about my people that make my heart sing.

Seeing Blackfellas and whitefellas working together to make a difference – it sounds so clichéd but – it's such a heartwarming sight. Whitefellas don't need to do this work like we do. They choose to get involved in reconciliation, and in making a difference for us they realise they get something special in return. And it makes a difference for them too.

And yet it's often Blackfellas who turn their noses up at the idea of reconciliation, whatever they think it means – some kind of sell-out I suppose. I've never felt that, nor did my Mother when she was criticised for getting involved.

My own natural optimism only wavers when I experience racism and when I sense the low expectations of my people, from others and from ourselves, particularly our young. The escalating violence in the world and in our communities. Inaction still by so many, or action that is disrespectful and manipulative, so destined to generate more failure. Sad things, and there are many, sharpen my conviction that for things to really change in this country, whitefellas have to come to terms with the racism too many of them will accept and excuse, even if they don't feel it themselves. Whitefellas need to look past their whiteness and try to feel what it is to 'walk a mile in our shoes'. There are no excuses any more for ignorance. There are so many opportunities to learn about our history through film and art and music, if it isn't from books or spoken word. Australia has a Black History, and the more Australians who learn it and take it in, the more who'll understand how it is for Aboriginal people.

And who will admire our resilience.

For Blackfellas what needs to change is being able to accept that reconciliation, however they imagine it – but let's define it as closing the life expectancy gap – was always going to be a two-way street. We have suffered terribly as a people, but in most cases now we have opportunities, choices that our parents and grandparents did not have. We need to make good choices.

I also think we can underestimate the amount of goodwill out there among whitefellas. From my experience, being able to trust white people, people who are worth trusting, developing relationships with them and letting them into our lives can be very liberating. I would never have said this in my younger days but I have changed in this process.

Being involved in reconciliation has brought me into contact with the best of people, both Black and white. Which is why my decision to retire from my formal role as Co-Chair of Reconciliation Australia at the end of the year feels very strange and already quite scary. But it's time for me to do other things, and time for someone else to come onto the Board of a top organisation.

My mentor and friend Fred Chaney helped me to make the call about retiring, and reaching 50 helped too. I admire the old Murries in my life and I want to live long enough to be one of them. I love the idea of growing older and wiser. Fred said I should 'go out on a high', and this anniversary year feels like a high to me.

It makes me feel that my life has come one full circle from the little girl who watched her Mother fight the battle in the early years. I've tried to be a leader like she was and I've been blessed to have been schooled by the best – Charlie Perkins, Captain Reg Saunders, Evelyn Scott and others who continue to inspire me. I hope I've repaid them.

I've had so many amazing experiences being involved in reconciliation. Most of them have been incredibly joyous. And a couple have been cripplingly awful. Like the time in 2000, a few weeks before the Bridge Walk in Sydney, when Evelyn Scott and I went to catch a cab in Pitt Street after a meeting.

People recognised Evelyn, she is always so well dressed. And I had on a lovely green suit. A cab came over the hill and pulled up, and when the driver got out, he completely ignored Evelyn and me even though we were pulling our luggage towards him. He called out 'Who is going to the airport?' and when we said we were he just kept ignoring us as though we weren't there.

It isn't a completely awful memory because a fellow standing in the queue challenged the driver about why he wasn't taking us. In fact all the people in the queue seemed horrified as they witnessed this racist act. And another man who'd come from further back in the queue asked whether the driver was refusing to take us. I just told him to get in because I knew if he didn't the driver would only drive off and find another fare who wasn't Black.

Another memory I often think about is working on the draft Declaration for Reconciliation in 2000 with the author David Malouf, who I admire so much. I'm so proud of what we came up with even though it hasn't been used as we'd hoped.

And there's the memory that makes me smile every time I think of it – the Bridge Walk in 2000. I'll never forget Sir Gus Nossal saying the day before, 'If there isn't 250,000 people walking, I'll be a monkey's Uncle.' Well, Gus was pretty well spot on according to official numbers. I still reckon it was more.

I have relished every minute of my thirteen-year involvement in reconciliation – the highs and the lows, walking three paces forward and two back, the magnificent and horrible people met along the way. It's been an unforgettable ride.

I hope I've made a good contribution. I've tried to. I know that I'm a much better and wiser person for having been involved.

I'm looking forward to spending more time at home and less on planes – although I'm sure I'll even miss that. More time with my loved ones who have had to get used to my absence over the years.

My professional plan is to concentrate on promoting leadership and education for my people. At home in Brisbane, I want to give back and support others who are striving to make a difference. I want to put back to my community the lessons learned in reconciliation over the years. I need to spend more time at The University of Queensland, my actual workplace, and where I was so grateful last year to receive an Honorary Doctorate.

I've been described in the past as a cross between a street fighter and a public intellectual, so I want to have the freedom to say things I want to say but feel I shouldn't say as Co-Chair of Reconciliation Australia, to take people on who insult my people.

That's how the new chapter looks from here, a few months out.

For now though, I am fully focused on next weekend and seeing the campaigners, linking up with people who fought the hard fight. Didn't hide their Aboriginality when there really was nothing in it for people to identify as being Black. Even some of our own relatives criticised us for being involved in the struggle for the Referendum. And after forty years, it's just so energising to revisit the stories and see how far we've come – to point out the glimpses of real progress in this journey called reconciliation.

It is, at its core, a liberation movement, reconciliation. Something that gives leaders an opportunity to lead and to take people along, as every good leader should.

As I hope I've done.

I will always think of reconciliation as a fine and noble cause to be involved in. I feel very lucky indeed to have been so closely involved with it for such a long, long time.

But this is a movement of today and the future, just as much as it is of the past. This week's anniversary is the right time for it to be imprinted on the nation's psyche as something we have to do.

Nobody questions whether a strong economy is a good thing. Nobody should doubt that reconciliation is in all of our best interests. Because it's right and because it's absolutely within our grasp.

Lowitja O'Donoghue Oration

It was an honour to give this oration in 2009 for one of the staunchest advocates of our times, Lowitja. She was on the Council for Aboriginal Reconciliation with me in 1995 along with other luminaries. I had followed her career for a long time and suddenly I was sitting in the same room as her! What an opportunity to observe her prowess and conviction. I said nothing for the first three years while on the council as I was overawed by her presence and that of the others. After every meeting I would pinch myself and ask, 'Was that all a dream?' Remembering my early days in Canberra in the 1970s as a typist/secretary and minute taker, watching my political heroes in action was something to behold. One day I would be sitting at the table with them I thought. My dream came true.

—

I wish to acknowledge the country of the Kaurna peoples of this land and thank them for the welcome and allowing me to speak on their country for what is the prestigious Lowitja O'Donoghue Oration, alongside my good friend Fred Chaney. I pay my respects to Elders past and present, and to all Aboriginal people within these boundaries.

In delivering this lecture 'Bringing Black and White Australians Together' I am reminded that I am often asked what does reconciliation mean to me. It means three things to me – Recognition, Justice and Healing.

Recognition as the First Peoples of this land, recognition that the First Australians should be included in the preamble of the Constitution and within the Constitution itself, and of course to be respected as such. We have existed here over 70,000 years and have maintained and cared for land and for people. There are moves to include this understanding from kindergarten level in the teaching of Aboriginal culture, which can only be hailed as a positive move. Far too long have we been asking our country to learn its true history.

Justice is about overcoming all the social disadvantages that can be summed up in one stunning statistic, which says our children can expect to die on average 11.8 years earlier than the children of other Australians. It has become a reality that when statistics are given about Aboriginal lives it is numbing and does not record in the psyche of most average Australians because the numbers are still so, so bad. However, I have absolutely no doubt that we can only meet this enormous challenge if we work together as Australians who care about it. That we work together with trust and with respect.

Healing because that really is our fundamental goal as human beings. And we will only achieve it in this country if we achieve reconciliation. But that will never be achieved if governments concentrate on 'practical reconciliation' and ignore the spiritual or symbolic side of reconciliation. By the symbolic, I mean all the many things that have to do with building respectful relationships. The balance needs to be right.

How can we share in this country's vast opportunity and prosperity if we don't understand the basic principle of respect in working together. It was something Australians understood in 1967 at the time of the Referendum, if only for a moment, but it has driven and inspired many people since, more and more people all the time. And not just a certain type of person, left leaning, religious, or just people who like stirring the pot.

Lots of different kinds of Australians support reconciliation. They're people who understand when something's not fair and know that something should be done about it. People in business, in government, in media, all different professions and political persuasions. People you meet in supermarkets.

People get involved because they feel something should be done about the disadvantage and maybe something can be done about it. They hear the good and the bad stuff and try to chip away at the misconceptions.

But getting there is going to require of us – First Peoples and others – that we shift out of our entrenched positions. We need to see and learn about what's actually working in improving Indigenous people's lives, and think about how we can reasonably apply it in different contexts. We need to be prepared to listen to one another.

Reconciliation started because enough Australian people wanted it.

There are many stories about Aboriginal and non-Aboriginal people working together. Perhaps more than we are prepared to realise. Thousands upon thousands upon thousands throughout our history. And when it got so hard these people would still stand shoulder to shoulder. People in the audience too, such as yourselves – you've all got a story for sure. People like you who have heard about various campaigns in your churches, women's groups, trade unions, and you'd tell your families, friends and workmates who then told their neighbours. For most of you, you decided to do something about it – even just coming here and listening to this oration is indeed involvement. It was many, many conversations that joined in a spirit of reconciliation and became a national determination. I know that kind of determination is still around today.

Seeing Blackfellas and whitefellas working together to make a difference – it sounds so clichéd but it's such a heartwarming sight. Whitefellas don't need to do this work like we do. They choose to get involved in reconciliation, and in making a difference for us they realise they get something special in return. And it makes a difference for them too.

My own natural optimism only wavers when I experience racism and when I sense the low expectations of my people, from others and from ourselves, particularly our young. The escalating violence and recession in the world and in our communities, inaction by so many, or action that is disrespectful and manipulative, are destined to generate failure.

Sad things, and there are many, sharpen my conviction that for the situation to really change in this country whitefellas have to come to terms with the racism too many of them will accept and excuse, even if they don't feel it themselves.

Being involved in reconciliation has brought me into contact with the best and worst of people – the highs and the lows, walking three paces forward and two back, the magnificent and horrible people met along the way. But somehow they bring out the best in the individual.

Australians need to know about these networks of change-makers who brought out the best in us. Because the best is always there waiting to be tapped by true leaders in our communities. True leaders like Lowitja O'Donoghue. No one knows the struggle better than Lowitja.

Then there is the leadership that has to happen at all levels of government and within our own communities. Throughout my time there have been so many influential leaders who have shone the light for First Australians. And then again there have been some who have done the opposite in relation to obstructing and denying a rightful place for Aboriginal and Torres Strait Islander peoples.

The work I currently do around leadership these days tells me that there is a great thirst out there among our people who want to do good things in their lives to get themselves and their communities into better shape. Research in other countries shows that leaders who got rid of their addictive behaviours and reliance on alcohol or drugs achieved outstanding results in their communities because their people wanted to follow them.

Great role models have paved the way for us and in my earlier life I was able to sit at the same table as people like Lowitja, Charles Perkins and many others whom I observed at close range the way they handled every type of situation. Their honesty and integrity in dealing with matters inspired me to do the same. And even my non-Aboriginal peers like Fred Chaney became the role models that I could borrow certain characteristics from to develop my unique style of leadership.

It isn't easy being a woman either, as Lowitja suggests:

I am always inspired by examples of people having the courage to act on what they know to be right. It sounds simple – but I believe that it is a rare quality in the contemporary economic and political landscape. It is difficult enough in any sphere for a woman to succeed in positions of leadership. I believe it is even more difficult for a woman in a leadership position. If she challenges the status quo and the values that drive and protect it. If she takes this role, she challenges both male power, and the systems that support and maintain it. (By definition she will be regarded as mad or bad – and sometimes both!)

Leaders need to be brave and have a vision. For Aboriginal people we are dictated to by our past and the legacy we carry on for our ancestors. The struggle is constant and burnout is a usual condition. For many of us we do so without thinking because this is our family that is at stake. The strategies applied after can have improved or drastic results.

Governments must listen to the solutions derived at the local level by Aboriginal and Torres Strait Islander people. There are many locally driven programs and other initiatives across the country that enable effective and creative solutions to be produced at the grassroots level.

A few weeks ago I attended the Indigenous Family Violence Prevention Forum held every year in Mackay for the Queensland Centre for Domestic and Family Violence Research which aims to:

- highlight and celebrate the good work that is being done by Aboriginal and Torres Strait Islander people to end family violence;
- share information and knowledge about strategies and programs that could be used effectively by others;
- promote opportunities for networking between workers in the field of family violence prevention; and
- identify issues to be addressed and recommend strategies to do so.

Each year, over 150 Aboriginal and Torres Strait Islander people from across the state, and more increasingly from interstate, come to tropical Mackay in Central Queensland for the forum, and to share their knowledge and expertise. Like all of the published research on family violence in communities, forum participants consistently put forward their strongly held views, based on their experience, that effective responses to domestic and family violence must be holistic, and locally developed, driven and owned. Policies and programs that are imposed on Aboriginal and Torres Strait Islander people are doomed to fail.

One of the ideas that came out of an early forum was the one at Woorabinda in Central Queensland, whereby footballers would be suspended from games if they engaged in any form of domestic or family violence. And further, would have to talk to school classes about why the violence is not acceptable. DV orders were reduced dramatically. Recently I have seen the same ideas meted out in some areas of New South Wales where football is popular in communities. Locally based solutions do actually work.

I take my hat off to the workers who work tirelessly at the coalface of such tragic areas. They do so with dedication and strength.

This year I have been involved with Tom Calma and others on the work on the National Representative Body Steering Committee to give our people a voice in national affairs and policy development. The Adelaide workshop saw a great deal of commitment from all participants who were keen on a positive direction for the future after a long hiatus in Aboriginal affairs. The consensus points reached included that it would be a self-determining and independent body that does not deliver services and has equal representation of men and women on the committee.

There was strong support for the representative body to primarily be an advocacy body and to focus on holding government to account for its performance in programs, service delivery and policy development. There was also a strong support for the body to have a direct relationship at a regional level so that its advocacy work is fully informed. Also, the new body would play a leading role in working to achieve constitutional recognition for Aboriginal and Torres Strait Islander peoples and helping to close the gap in health status within a generation.

There was consensus that the representative body should play a unifying role among communities and contribute to Aboriginal and Torres Strait Islander people controlling their own destiny and being economically independent. Workshop participants agreed the new body should have mechanisms in place to ensure the participation of people who are generally marginalised in representative processes, such as young people, people with disability, members of the Stolen Generation and mainland Torres Strait Islanders. It would also represent the diversity of peoples in terms of geographical locations, relations to country and cultural diversity.

There have been many key issues for me in reconciliation overall, however it has been about how we build a respectful relationship between everyone that is foremost. How do we accomplish that in our continuing journey? The issue was how to get across what a dignified race of people we actually are – to look at the rich culture that we come from, the old and ancient culture, and how to encompass that in the fabric of Australian society, how to make it fundamentally the focus, the basis by which we are all here today. So it's about understanding and knowing, coming to terms with the beautiful culture we have in our country.

One of the ways we can stay positive is to look at the workable and successful programs we have around the country which concentrate on the positives and derive their existence around the good and not the bad. Starting off where people are at rather than seeing them as hapless victims who don't deserve a second chance. We just never hear enough good stories but we know there are so many.

I am privileged in that I work with the cream of the crop at Queensland University. Our students, who are not without their struggles too, sit in classes day in and day out to achieve the qualifications that can get them a better future and perhaps one in which their grandparents and parents could never imagine. I see our young women studying engineering, our young men aerodynamics and physics, and it is truly astounding. Perhaps I do work in an environment that doesn't lend itself to too many failures or you're out, but nevertheless they are there.

A researcher asked me recently if reconciliation had 'lost its hour'! I am still not sure what she meant by that but I responded by saying that I am a Leo and by nature very optimistic and showy. I don't know where I would be or where this country would be if we never had a reconciliation plan in place. I fear a place without it, no matter how tangible that place is. There has been change and when you have been a part of that change it is very hard to go back to thinking there has been little change. We've all worked so hard for it that hopefully our lives have been for something. So by no means has it vanished, I told her, except we just need some oxygen masks from time to time, boosters to help us get to the next level and some soothers when we fall to get up again and keep trying.

I will always think of reconciliation as a fine and noble cause to be involved in. The art of Black and white working together is something I saw as a child when my Mother was politically active and the good people we associated with who saw our treatment as shameful and who were prepared to do something about it. That is seen today and I can never give up on it. It's part of my DNA. I feel very lucky to have been so closely involved with it for such a long time.

But this is a movement of today and the future, just as much as it is of the past. More than ever we need Black and white working together in unison. It is only then can we really make the difference.

National Congress of Australia's First Peoples

One of the pinnacles of my life was being elected the Co-Chair of the National Congress of Australia in 2015. Years before this I was fortunate to be involved in its formation. I gave this speech in Sydney on 7 June 2011 when I was on the Steering Committee. Sadly our organisation had a short life, surviving on drip feed from the federal government. I believe it was far too ahead of its time. Whitefellas and Blackfellas didn't get it. Certainly the government policy makers and bureaucrats did not make it easy for us. Hostile politicians from the prime minister down never understood its authenticity or power. Maybe the new representative Voice which is currently being proposed will be able to benefit from lessons learnt and opportunities missed.

———

Let me start by acknowledging we meet on the land of the Waan-Gal people.

I am excited to be here today to speak on behalf of the Steering Committee that contributed to the development of the National Congress of Australia's First Peoples. The journey to get here has been long, it has been frustrating, it has been challenging, yet somehow, it has even been entertaining at times. The stories I could tell you ...

Of course today isn't a time to relive every minor detail of the journey behind us. I want to spend most of the short time I have to speak with you about my aspirations for this national body, and expectations of how I believe we should work together. I want to talk about the kind of leadership we need, the standard of leadership we deserve, and the strength of leadership we must demand in this new organisation. But to put this into context, I do feel it is important to point out some of what I have learnt and some of what we experienced along the way.

Firstly, I have to say, without question, it has been an absolute privilege to contribute to the development and design of the Congress. I stand by our processes and I know we listened to all the views that were put before us given the limitations of time and resources we had to work with. We considered the input from previous processes and we even tried to make sense of the views of those brothers and sisters who gave support, encouragement and advice in person, and then relayed completely opposite views and a complete lack of support in the media. We tried to understand it all.

You will probably remember back in 2004, the Howard government decided to abolish ATSIC. The writing had been on the wall for some time so it was not so much shocking as it was predictable. However, it was sudden and executed with little notice. As a member of the review panel I was shocked.

Within five days of the announcement I was involved in a meeting initiated by Reconciliation Australia. There were only fifteen or so of us there although I understand folklore suggests there were at least thirty of us. We talked, argued and debated the consequences of a life without a national representative body. We considered the reasons why this had happened so brutally and how we found ourselves in this position with little left to help us organise a co-ordinated national and collective voice. Typically, we concluded that meeting with an agreement to hold another meeting with more people.

In just under four weeks, we managed to raise the money and organise a four-day meeting in Adelaide with from between 200 and 400 participants on any one day.

For the next twelve months we tried to engage people in consultations about starting a new national representative body. However, most people were focusing on trying to establish and maintain regional structures and funding for services. It was a difficult time and government seemed to be successful at keeping us apart and disorganised at the national level.

Despite this, there were fundraising efforts to run a thorough and appropriate national consultation process on a new body. We sought funds from philanthropic friends and kindly corporates who confessed an interest in supporting us to get a new credible national voice in place. Submissions were written, meetings had, and every lead chased.

But when it came down to it, those who professed a desire to see us back on our collective national feet found reasons to deny us support. Ultimately they had no confidence in our ability to form a national body that would be functional and make a tangible difference. They didn't trust an agenda led by us alone. In short, they would provide money if we did it their way and on their terms. The truth is, our potential funders just did not believe we could build a credible, legitimate and effective body.

I'm telling this part of the story because you need to know government was not the first place we went to when trying to secure resources to build this organisation. It was a last resort, and even that came as a result of lobbying with the then opposition.

That brought us into the process that was led by Tom Calma and consolidated years of effort to bring us to this inaugural Congress of Australia's First Peoples. Tom has already covered the background and process that built on the early work that brings us here today so I want to move on to the elements of the model of this organisation that have probably resulted in the greatest criticism.

Let's be clear, the Ethics Council was devised to address the concerns we heard constantly about the danger of the organisation losing credibility and legitimacy because of the poor judgement or poor leadership of a few. We heard strong support for this at the Adelaide workshop in 2009 and through focus groups, consultations and in some of the written submissions. We supported this notion not to appease or satisfy the lack of faith by non-Indigenous Australia but because people who participated in our process made it clear that we must accept nothing but the best standard of leadership possible, ethically and morally.

There was never a desire to try and create an elite demographic profile for the organisation but to provide a mechanism for our people to deal with our own matters on our terms and by our own standards and drawing on our community wisdom and integrity.

Secondly, and I am particularly proud of this initiative, the governance model for this organisation will ensure women are never denied a voice. It does not matter to me that the rest of the country doesn't employ this basic principle of gender equity but I am extremely proud that it is our organisation that is leading the way on this. The rest of Australia may not do it. I believe it is right that we do and it is a direct demonstration that we know our organisation will be weaker if we don't ensure men and women lead and are equally accountable. Even the Sex Discrimination Commissioner, Liz Broderick, hailed our model as groundbreaking, whereby all Australian institutions to lead by this example.

This may be a new approach but I firmly believe that any leader worthy of this organisation will find a way to make this approach work. This initiative is around cultural integrity that dates back to our ancestors in reinstating and deploying men's business and women's business again. True governance cannot operate without it and that is why some of our organisations fail. Our women everywhere are now demanding equal partnership to work alongside our men.

I feel so optimistic about what this new body can achieve, we have a clean slate, and we can build a new foundation to really improve our status, our recognition and rights as the First Peoples of this country. I have great expectations of the leadership moving forward.

It is going to take a lot of different people, skills and attributes to make this organisation successful and strong. Quality, integrity and accountability in our leadership will always be important and that will be my most basic expectation of those who step forward to lead.

As I said at the beginning of this speech, this has been a long and difficult journey but I am proud of the work we have done. I am proud that the organisation has been established and we have a model that will not allow the voices of women (and I hope children) to be diminished.

I am proud to have been part of a committee that was prepared to make decisions, even when those decisions had to be made in less than ideal circumstances. I can tell you, there were many teleconferences conducted with crying children, barking dogs and The Wiggles as our soundtrack. Parts of the constitution were mapped out on serviettes in hotel lobbies. Not ideal but sometimes that just had to do.

I am proud of the younger people who have stepped up to make invaluable contributions to building this organisation that will carry our hopes and aspirations. And as I take my Senior status seriously these days I am happy to sit back, watch and guide if needed.

I am proud of the potential before us to build a body that is strong, independent and smart.

Finally, it is my sincere hope that I will continue to feel this pride in this organisation. I want to feel proud of the leadership we elect. Pride in an organisation that is focused on what is important, rather than only what is popular.

I have big expectations for this body to lead us well, strongly and with integrity. I expect the organisation to build the membership, and listen to the membership.

I don't expect to always agree with the decisions that are taken but I expect to be consulted about the direction and priorities. I expect the organisation to be inclusive, strategic, smart and ambitious for our people.

Finally, I want to sincerely thank you, Dr Tom Calma, for your leadership of the process. It was a wonderful experience we shared and your leadership and commitment was critical to this success we have achieved to date. I also want to acknowledge the other Steering Committee members who stayed the course and who believed we could establish and run a long-awaited, effective national organisation. It's been a hard voluntary exercise but just look around us – how exciting is this?

This is my final duty as a former Steering Committee member and I look forward to stepping back into delegate mode and working with you all at this historic first inaugural Congress and in the years to come.

Thank you.

Commemorative Address, Remembrance Day

The rainy day on Remembrance Day 2015 belied the historical event which was about to occur. Sentiment and history poured down as I proudly gave the Commemorative Address at the Australian War Memorial in Canberra, the first Indigenous person, non politician, non military, or public official to do so in history. Many dignitaries were in attendance including the Governor General, Prince Charles and Camilla, the Prime Minister, Opposition Leader, Chief of the Australian Defence Force and other distinguished guests. Did I have a story to tell them all. I have considered myself a child of many wars, both recognised and not, and a descendant of brave soldiers – my Father and Grandfather in World War I and World War II.

—

I commence by paying my respects to the Traditional Owners, the Ngunnawal peoples, their Elders, past, present and future.

I also pay my respects to the past and present Aboriginal and Torres Strait Islander men and women who enlisted, and who served in an auxiliary capacity for the Australian Defence Forces, and to all Australians who have given their lives for us in war and in peace.

Among them, we are especially mindful of the families of the forty-two men who gave their lives for our nation in Afghanistan who are with us here today.

I am deeply appreciative of the opportunity to address you today on an occasion that resonates through our collective memories.

The Australian War Memorial is a sacred place to all Australians.

In this centenary year of the Gallipoli landings and all that followed, Remembrance Day 2015 assumes an even more poignant meaning.

World War I remains Australia's greatest modern tragedy – almost 62,000 dead, another 60,000 dying within a decade of their return and many more injured, maimed and psychologically scarred.

Few families, mine included, were untouched by its horror.

My name is Jackie Huggins, and I am a Bidjara and Birri Gubba Juru woman from Queensland.

My family proudly served this nation – *our* nation in both world wars.

Like many others touched by the evacuation of Gallipoli, my Grandfather John Huggins enlisted in December 1915 from Charters Towers, embarking from Brisbane on HMAT *Seang Choon* A49 on the 4th of May 1916.

Grandfather was a superb stockman and would have loved to continue his craft and ride horses overseas. Unfortunately, he was not assigned to the Light Horse Brigade.

Private Huggins was first sent to Egypt, where he continued his training with the 9th Battalion, and then to England, where he was posted to the 3rd Training Battalion. On the 3rd of December 1916, after arriving in France, Huggins was transferred to the 26th Battalion where he remained for the rest of his service. The 26th Battalion was part of the 7th Brigade of the 2nd Division.

Grandfather was wounded in Belgium on the 4th of October 1917 during the bloody battle of Broodseinde. As the 26th

Battalion came over Broodseinde Ridge they encountered heavy fire from snipers and enemy machine guns situated in concrete bunkers known as pillboxes. He suffered a gunshot wound to the left forearm. He was evacuated to England on the HS *Pieter de Cornick* and admitted to Norfolk and Norwich Hospital, and later to Norfolk War Hospital.

In March 1918 the 26th Battalion went into the frontline near the Belgian town of Ploegsteert. Private Huggins was wounded for the second time, suffering a gunshot wound to the leg. He was evacuated to the military hospital in Bethnal Green, London, and from there was repatriated to Australia on board HMAT *Saxon*.

My Father – also named John Huggins – was born in Ayr, North Queensland, in 1920. To those of us who knew and loved him, he was 'Jack' – a man of high degree, compassion and integrity.

This was a different Australia from the one we are today.

Despite the class and racial barriers of the time, he was the first Indigenous Australian to serve in the Australian Post Office. He was a surf lifesaver and a fervent 'A grade' Rugby League player. Like his Father before him, he understood that serving his country and his nation was a privilege.

My Father enlisted in the Second AIF on 27 March 1941 in Ayr, joining the 2/29th Battalion, which was part of the 27th Brigade of the 8th Division.

The 27th Brigade was the last AIF infantry brigade raised for service during the World War II. It fell to the Japanese in February 1942 after the fierce defence of Singapore. The 2/29th Battalion spent three and a half years as prisoners of war, first concentrated in Changi prison.

As one of the fittest soldiers, Dad was sent to the horror that was building the Thai–Burma Railway. Japanese engineers estimated that the railway, to be built through dense jungle and mountain, would take five years to construct and required thousands of engineers and labourers. Instead it took under a year, using starved, diseased and beaten POW labour. Sadly and ironically the railway was completed in mid-October 1943, but it was never used. Almost as soon as it was completed it was damaged by Allied bombing. Today only sections of it survive.

An only child, my Father adored his Mother and Father.

The saddest moment of his life was when he arrived in Townsville after returning from the war. As my Father got off the train, weak, emaciated and tired, he scanned around for his Mother and wondered why she had not written to him for a few months since his liberation. On the platform he was told the tragic news by a good mate – she had died three months earlier.

He collapsed in his friend's arms. His Father had died earlier in 1942. Neither knew their beloved son survived the brutal horrors of the Thai–Burma Railway.

When my Father returned to civilian life, he did not experience the invisibility and exclusion dished out to many other Aboriginal service people. Aboriginal and Torres Strait Islander veterans were often denied the honour and rights given to other veterans, such as soldier settlement land grants. Many were refused membership, even entrance to RSL clubs.

As a prominent member of the local community, my Father was welcomed at the Ayr RSL club where he enjoyed a drink or two. He sought comfort in the POW Association where those who had experienced the terrors of captivity, starvation and unrelenting work could feel fully understood and accepted.

It was not until 1962 that all Indigenous peoples were granted full Australian citizenship.

Like others, my Father died at the age of 38 from complications of his war injuries. I was only 2 years old. I mourn his loss and the emptiness in my heart every day.

My Father and Grandfather, along with many other Indigenous men and women, served our nation in war.

Yet the dispossession, beginning in 1788, had destroyed their ancient civilisation.

However their abiding loyalty to this country we all call home, rose above the deep bitterness of the past. These men and women forged new identities that challenged the haunting devastations wrought by widespread violent colonial brutality and heralded a new and different future for us all.

On this historic occasion here at the Australian War Memorial, we honour and remember with pride, all those Australians who served our nation, and all those families like mine, that have so loved and supported them.

Prejudice versus Racism: Exploring the Comfort Zone

Public orations can be boring or interesting, nevertheless they are important in conveying direct messages to the audience, wider public, politicians, media etc. In my case, doing the annual Kep Enderby Lecture 'Prejudice versus Racism: Exploring the Comfort Zone' in 2016 was a way to do this. This lecture honoured a long time social justice advocate in the fields of law and human rights. His family were present so I knew I had to do a good job. I explored a number of past and present topics in the hour I was allocated such as those below. In fact I knew I wasn't boring as I received a standing ovation that night.

—

I acknowledge the Aboriginal people and Torres Strait Islander people who are not only the rightful owners of this continent, but who are the spiritual and inherent guardians of the living landscape. We will always be the heart and soul of Australia and I pay my respects to the Traditional Owners of this land – the Gadigal people of the Eora nation and their Elders past and present.

I pay my respects to Uncle Allen Madden, Keir Enderby (Kep Enderby's son) and his wife, Rosemary Enderby. I also congratulate Kupa Matangira for receiving the Student Essay

Prize this evening. While I know she couldn't be here tonight, I acknowledge the first woman Aboriginal and Torres Strait Islander Social Justice Commissioner and Bunuba woman, June Oscar. I warmly acknowledge Race Discrimination Commissioner Dr Tim Soutphommasane and the dedicated and vital work of the Australian Human Rights Commission.

Aboriginal and Torres Strait Islander people across Australia fight every day to keep our families together; to assert our rights and to uphold our cultures. I recognise our struggles, resilience and strength.

I also acknowledge the non-Indigenous people who have stood resolutely beside Aboriginal and Torres Strait Islander people and defended our rights. People who have shared stories of the inequality we face; who have called out racism; who have protected our rights. I thank you for standing with our First Peoples.

We must always draw on the strengths of those who have come before us. Our recently passed great champion, Dr Evelyn Scott, who took to heart her Father's words: 'If you don't think something is right, then challenge it.'

Keppel Earl Enderby QC did that, and tonight I honour him for it.

Recognition of Kep Enderby
In this third oration in honour of Kep Enderby, I am privileged to reflect on his contributions to not only the Australian legal and political systems, but also to the human rights framework upon which my people have often fiercely gripped.

Kep Enderby was an accomplished and passionate Australian, committed to civil liberty and law reform. He campaigned for gay rights, abortion rights and was fiercely opposed to poker machines. He was involved in reforming the Trade Practices Act and the Family Law Act and the introduction of legal aid. While serving as head of the Serious Offenders Review Council in New South Wales between 1997 and 2000, he was outspoken against the manipulation of public hysteria about crime and the consequent rising rates of imprisonment.

As Attorney-General for the Commonwealth, he introduced into the Parliament the Bill that became the *Racial Discrimination Act 1975* (Cth) (RDA) and came into force on this day, October 31st, of that same year.

The RDA is a foundational piece of legislation establishing Australia's identity as a nation upholding equality and tolerance within a diverse multicultural society. It is also a keystone for reconciliation in Australia between Aboriginal and Torres Strait Islander peoples and non-Indigenous people.

The RDA gave domestic effect to Australia's international obligations under the International Convention on the Elimination of All Forms of Racial Discrimination. The Act featured prominently in the Mabo decision of the High Court in 1992. On a number of occasions it has also prevented state governments from creating laws discriminating against Aboriginal and Torres Strait Islander peoples.

The strength of the RDA was tested recently when the Coalition Government attempted to remove or water down the protections provided against racial vilification – section 18C.

The RDA has not always stood as an unwavering pillar of our protection. The application of it was suspended in the Northern Territory to allow the roll-out of some elements of the intervention. The suspension of the RDA was widely criticised, including by the Law Council of Australia, which described the move as 'utterly unacceptable' and 'in direct and unashamed contravention of Australia's obligations under relevant international instruments'.[1] Further, the United Nations Human Rights Committee stated in its 2009 report on Australia's performance under the International Declaration on Civil and Political Rights that it was 'particularly concerned at the negative impact of the NTER measures on the enjoyment of the rights of Indigenous peoples and at the fact that they suspend the operation of the RDA and were adopted without adequate consultation with the Indigenous peoples.'[2]

Racism

Tonight, I acknowledge that it has also been an incredibly troubling year when we consider *Aboriginal and Torres Strait Islander children*. I want to acknowledge the work of the Royal Commission into the Protection and Detention of Children in the Northern Territory for its ability to tell the stories of our children whom this Country has failed. The Commission has collected the voices of our most vulnerable and tells of their capture, imprisonment and inhumane treatment – stories which should not exist. I respect the pain that this work brings to the surface for all involved and I honour the importance of sharing it with the broader community.

'We know from the work in the Lowitja Institute that racism, indeed makes us sick.'[3] And yet, the 2016 Australian Reconciliation Barometer found that 37 per cent of Aboriginal and Torres Strait Islander Australians have experienced verbal racial abuse in the last six months. This compares with 31 per cent in 2014.[4]

The right to be free from discrimination is recognised in Article 2 of the United Nations Declaration on the Rights of Indigenous Peoples, which Australia endorsed in 2009:

Indigenous peoples and individuals are free and equal to all other peoples and individuals and have the right to be free from any kind of discrimination, in the exercise of their rights, in particular that based on their Indigenous origin or identity.

For the majority of last century we lived under a regime which identified the colour of skin as the licence to acceptance and to citizenship: the White Australia Policy. Other racist and destructive measures existed, including the Stolen Generation; the forced removal of our people from their lands; relocation of our people to reservations and missions; assimilation; stolen wages; and the Northern Territory Intervention, which continues to operate under the guise of the 'Stronger Futures' policy.

These policies have caused ongoing sorrow and intergenerational trauma. The destruction of land, sacred sites, cultures and languages, coupled with racial discrimination have often led some of our people to feel as if their lives are worthless. These policies continue to haunt our people.

As Paul Keating reminded us all in 1992:

We took the traditional lands and smashed the traditional way of life. We brought the diseases. The alcohol. We committed the murders. We took the children from their mothers. We practised discrimination and exclusion. It was our ignorance and our prejudice. And our failure to imagine these things being done to us.[5]

The practice of discrimination and exclusion remains today. Some of our people are still kept apart from us – by politics and power – and forced to live away from the people who care most about them. They are in prisons and in out-of-home care. As long as they exist separated from us, from their families, from our communities and from our society, we remain a people who are unable to exercise *the right of self-determination*.[6] We remain people who are *discriminated against on the basis of race*.

We make up 2.8 per cent of the Australian population, but more than 25 per cent of the prison population. Imprisonment rates are even worse for Aboriginal and Torres Strait Islander young people, who represent 50 per cent of the youth prison population.

Twenty years after the 'Bringing Them Home' report was

handed down in 1997, our Aboriginal and Torres Strait Islander children are still being removed from their homes and, alarmingly, at even greater rates than ever before. In 1997, SNAICC – the National Voice for Our Children – submitted to the report that the 'critical principle of the right to self-determination has been all but ignored and swept under the carpet in relation to Aboriginal families and children'. Disturbingly, we can utter those same words today twenty years later.

Tonight I acknowledge the Aboriginal and Torres Strait Islander women – our Mothers, Sisters, daughters, nurturers and leaders – who are distraught in prisons, torn away from their families and children. Ninety per cent of them have been victims of violence or sexual assault, and 80 per cent of them are mothers. They make up 33 per cent of the female prison population in Australia.

Ms Dhu was one of them. A 22-year-old Yamatji woman, imprisoned for unpaid fines. Three days later, Ms Dhu died an agonising death in police custody from injuries she sustained due to domestic violence. Three years after her death, and following a coronial inquest, the Western Australian government has still not implemented key findings made by the coroner.

Months after the initiation of the Royal Commission into the Protection and Detention of Children in the Northern Territory, a 10-year-old Aboriginal boy has been seen handcuffed to two police officers while on a plane from Mount Isa to Townsville.

Our First People continue to lose their lives, alone in prison cells. Our children continue to be abused at the hands of the legal system and its institutions.

I hate racial discrimination most intensely and all its manifestations. I have fought it all my life; I fight it now, and will do until the end of my days.[7]

These words belong to Nelson Mandela, but they may have been spoken by many of our First Peoples.

The Uluru Statement from the Heart

The Uluru Statement from the Heart is a call for a genuine representative body and treaties process. It is a call to the nation to honour the sovereignty of our people. To address the 'torment of our powerlessness'.[8]

It spoke to substantive constitutional change and structural reform. The Makarrata Commission seeks 'to supervise a process of agreement-making between governments and First Nations and truth-telling about our history'.[9]

> Makarrata is the culmination of our agenda: *the coming together after a struggle*. It captures our aspirations for a fair and truthful relationship with the people of Australia and a better future for our children based on justice and self-determination.[10]

National Congress is the voice for Aboriginal and Torres Strait Islander Australia. We were very disappointed by the events in Canberra last week which dismissed the historic and comprehensive process of the Uluru Convention and the Statement. So many people have worked very hard for many years to tackle these issues, and it felt to many Indigenous people that our aspirations were disparagingly sidelined.

National Congress will continue to work with all political parties to ensure that the call for a Makarrata Commission is honoured.

We will also continue to advocate for the removal of racially discriminatory provisions within the Australian Constitution.

Section 51 (xxvi) of the Constitution allows the Parliament to pass laws that can discriminate against any Australian *on the basis of race.*

Section 25 contemplates the possibility that states can ban people from voting *on the basis of race.*

While these provisions exist, we as a nation are *accepting racism.*

As Senator Dodson said:

Freedom, Peace and Justice are values that are universally yearned for by all peoples. Their absence in the lives of individuals, communities and nations clearly *diminishes us all if we stand by and do nothing.*[11]

Australia's failings under the International Human Rights Framework

National Congress of Australia's First Peoples advocates self-determination and the implementation of the United Nations Declaration on the Rights of Indigenous Peoples. We believe that Aboriginal and Torres Strait Islander people should be central in decisions about our lives and communities, and in all areas including our lands, health, education, law, governance, and economic empowerment.

We promote respect for our cultures and recognition as the core of the national heritage.

Despite committing itself to implementing the United Nations Declaration on the Rights of Indigenous Peoples at the World Conference on Indigenous Peoples in 2014, the Australian Government has resisted adopting many international recommendations that would assist it in doing so. These include legal provisions to prevent the enactment of discriminatory laws and a plan of action for supporting our rights.

The government is yet to take steps recommended by the former Special Rapporteur on the Rights of Indigenous Peoples, Mr James Anaya, to ensure that our communities are not exploited by extractive industries and other corporations. And it has not responded to the report on Australia by the current UN Special Rapporteur on the Rights of Indigenous Peoples, Ms Victoria Tauli-Corpuz, handed down earlier this year.

Despite repeated calls for self-determination from the Aboriginal and Torres Strait Islander community, the Australian Government continues to pursue paternalistic policies which prevent us from attaining self-governance.

The 2007 Northern Territory Intervention is one of the most recent and devastating examples of non-negotiated, racist commonwealth intervention into the lives of Aboriginal people. It was a deeply hurtful and poorly administered attempt to *label* our people as shameful – and it was done for political electoral gain.

The continuation of the Northern Territory Intervention under the new brand of the Stronger Futures policy has led to over-policing in our communities; the forced participation in work for the dole schemes which pay individuals far less than the minimum wage; and the perpetuation of stigma against us. As Senator Patrick Dodson has said:

No one denies the need to address the issues confronting the Aboriginal people all over Australia. But the failure by the Government to enter into a dialogue and negotiation over the nature of the engagement with the Aboriginal society of the Northern Territory will be seen by Australians in the future as a model for worst practice imposition of public policy and a further addition to the litany of administrative disasters that gave us the Stolen Generations.[12]

Although the Native Title Act provides some protections for our land, native title has been significantly weakened through successive government policies and High Court rulings. Pastoral leases extinguish native title where there is a conflict of rights, and corporate and political interests regularly take precedence over our connection to land, as demonstrated in the controversy surrounding the construction of the Hindmarsh Island Bridge.

Australia's development policies for Aboriginal and Torres Strait Islander communities continue to be assimilationist in nature. The Community Development Program has forced many individuals into forms of employment with little cultural relevance to us. Although some health and education outcomes have improved, a lack of culturally appropriate services and bilingual teaching has stymied progress in these areas.

The reorganisation of development funding under the Indigenous Advancement Strategy has led to the collapse of small Aboriginal and Torres Strait Islander organisations unable to engage in competitive bidding processes and the inflation of bureaucratic costs.

Political parties do not rely on *our* vote to win elections, but perhaps they rely on the racist psyche of some members of the Australian population to use us as social experiments.

The cashless debit card, which has been trialled in two locations of predominantly Aboriginal welfare recipients,[13] is yet another example of such an experiment. The Debit Card Bill repackages the worst aspects of the income management policy introduced with the Northern Territory Emergency Response, continued with the 'BasicsCard' in the Stronger Futures package and the 'Healthy Welfare Card' proposed by The Forrest Review.

The cashless debit card similarly continues to punish the majority for the problems of the few; exacerbates perceptions of disempowerment; and encourages discrimination by government authorities toward Aboriginal and Torres Strait Islander peoples.

The Way Forward

National Congress urges the federal government to revisit the statements made by Prime Minister Malcolm Turnbull at the

Closing the Gap speech to parliament in 2016:

> A few weeks after I became the Prime Minister, I crossed paths with Dr Chris Sarra. I asked him what three things we could do in Indigenous policy that would truly make a difference ... This is what he said: Firstly, acknowledge, embrace and celebrate the humanity of Indigenous Australians. Secondly, bring us policy approaches that nurture hope and optimism rather than entrench despair. And lastly, do things with us, not to us.[14]

We have endured decades of reports and reviews and enquiries that have captured the racist experiences of our people:

- Bringing Them Home
- Little Children are Sacred
- The Royal Commission into Aboriginal Deaths in Custody
- Unfinished Business.

There are hundreds of recommendations within these documents that are yet to be implemented.

How do we bestow the future to our children with a promise that their lives won't be haunted based on their race? That they will not suffer the trauma of mistreatment by police and politicians? That their children won't fill Australia's prisons or be ripped away from their families in unprecedented numbers?

In the words of Galarrwuy Yunupingu:

> What Aboriginal people ask is that the modern world now makes the sacrifices necessary to give us a real future. To relax its grip on us. To let us breathe, to let us be free of the

determined control exerted on us to make us like you. And you should take that a step further and recognise us for who we are, and not who you want us to be. Let us be who we are – Aboriginal people in a modern world – and be proud of us. Acknowledge that we have survived the worst that the past had thrown at us, and we are here with our songs, our ceremonies, our land, our language and our people – our full identity. What a gift this is that we can give you, if you choose to accept us in a meaningful way.[15]

This NAIDOC Week, I Want to Acknowledge My Sisters in Jail

Every year NAIDOC and National Reconciliation Week come and go but some players remain the same, stuck in isolation, missing their children and families. These are the incarcerated women who deserve much more attention. Not to mention the women who have died in custody. Sisters Inside, ably run by Debbie Kilroy, is the primary source of inspiration and assistance to the women who languish in jail, largely for minor offences. During my life I have had women community and family members behind bars and when the prison doors shut it is an eerie feeling. We sometimes invisible the visible and I delivered this piece for them in July 2018.

——

I am unbelievably proud to be an Aboriginal woman.

I feel an enormous sense of privilege to be part of such an intricate and ancient culture. We are the oldest known continuing culture on this planet.

The theme of this year's NAIDOC Week is 'Because of Her, We Can!' It has been heartwarming to celebrate the many female Aboriginal and Torres Strait Islander role models, and to hear stories about women answering the call and generating meaningful social change for First Peoples.

On hearing these stories, I can't help but think of my Sisters who are in jail. Although we represent 3 per cent of the Australian population, Aboriginal and Torres Strait Islander women make up 34 per cent of the female prison population. We are twenty-one times more likely to be imprisoned than non-Indigenous women.

First Women are the fastest growing prison demographic in the country, if not the world. We have seen a 148 per cent increase in our women being imprisoned since the Royal Commission into Aboriginal Deaths in Custody in 1991.

This week has showcased the incredible strength of Aboriginal and Torres Strait Islander women. Many of these women have overcome significant challenges to go on and achieve great things.

It saddens me to think about what our women in jail could have achieved if they had not been systematically failed by Australian society.

Many people think that if someone commits a crime, then imprisonment is justified: 'Aboriginal and Torres Strait Islander peoples are not in jail for nothing.' I wonder if these people know that the majority of people who are in jail have not been sentenced. I wonder if these people know about the scores of Aboriginal and Torres Strait Islander people in jail for unpaid fines, often for minor traffic offences, such as driving without a licence. (To get a licence, you need a birth certificate, which costs money. Then you need a licenced driver who has the time to supervise you for 120 hours. Not to mention the cost of petrol. This is near impossible in many remote Aboriginal communities.)

I wonder if these people know the social determinants of criminality. The Australian Institute of Health and Welfare found that two in three prison entrants had used illicit drugs in the year before their imprisonment. I was saddened but not surprised to learn that two in three prison entrants had not studied past Year 10 at school.

Research has demonstrated a clear link between child sexual assault, drug addiction and criminality for First Women in jail. A study on Aboriginal women in NSW prisons found that a staggering 70 per cent had experienced child abuse, 70 per cent had been sexually assaulted as children and 75 per cent were victims of domestic violence.

My guess is that very few people know these things. The level of ignorance among the Australian population about the challenges facing Aboriginal and Torres Strait Islander peoples never ceases to amaze me. It is this ignorance which fuels the astounding racism and lack of empathy from mainstream society towards First Peoples.

It saddens me to think of the intergenerational impact of incarceration. Eight per cent of First Women in jail are mothers. The imprisonment of these women continues the cycle of family and cultural breakdown and destruction.

Children with a parent who has been incarcerated are at risk of poor development in all areas, even after controlling for sociodemographic factors – parent's criminalisation is an independent risk factor for development.

Research has revealed that these impacts are exacerbated when it is the mother who is incarcerated. Imprisoning mothers makes it even harder to overcome already significant social and economic challenges for our children. In many cases, imprisonment of a parent makes it near impossible to break the cycle of criminality and poverty.

Australian society is both criminalising and entrenching poverty, abuse and disadvantage through mass incarceration.

It costs the Australian government $110,000 to imprison one person for one year. And Australia's prisoner population is skyrocketing. More and more money is being funnelled into prison infrastructure.

Public opinion that sentencing is too lenient has fuelled our nation's punitive turn. 'Tough on crime' policies such as mandatory minimum sentencing win votes.

We are spending $4 billion per year on the prison system. And this system is systematically failing to reform people, creating what Andrew Bushnell has termed a 'class of persistent criminals'.

This is shockingly ineffective economic and social policy. Imagine if even a fraction of that $4 billion was put into preventive policies that address the root causes of criminality and stopped people from offending in the first place.

The most effective policy solutions to challenges facing Indigenous peoples are those designed, led, implemented and evaluated by Indigenous peoples. Funding community-controlled organisations to target the social determinants of criminality would save the government a huge amount in the long run.

This NAIDOC week, spare a thought for First Women in jail. Think of what they could have achieved if they could fulfil their potential and contribute to society. Imagine if these women could be the mothers they wanted to be, to successfully grow up their children and children's children, then it would be quite a different story.

Building more prisons is not the solution.

These families need support. Our women in jail need support. We have the solutions. Please listen to us.

Don't Call Me Aunty

When age 50 came around I was suddenly identified as 'Aunty' to all and sundry. I thought one day I am going to write an essay that dispels the myths and stereotypes about objectifying this glorious, yet so often used, inappropriate term. Fifteen years later, in 2021, here it is. This my personal preference to set the record straight, knowing that it does not apply to all Aboriginal women. I base my objections in this piece on race, class and age. I am writing this for my Sister Girls who are sadly labelled with this tag from often well-intentioned people and have often succumbed to the pressure of it all. Next time show them this article, my Tiddas.

———

So let's begin with where my Aunty journey first started. I became a toddler Aunty at 3 years of age when my Big Sister, Marian aka Mutoo Holt/Chapman/Arnold, produced a beautiful daughter called Rosie. Sadly both are no longer with us, passing away far too young. However both left indelible legacies in their huge families of children and grandchildren.

In cultural terms Rosie and her sibling's children call me Nan or Gran, as I am their Grandmother's Sister. My Cherbourg/Murgon family of my Big Sister's got it right. I now have great-great-grandchildren through her line.

Rosie was my first blood-niece and named after my maternal Grandmother. Throughout my life I was always called Aunty by family members, which is the case in our Indigenous world. I loved my sacred ascription of Aunty at such a young age. It made me feel so special, worthy and responsible.

Of course, not to call me Aunty when related is a high mark of disrespect. Our Elders would chastise my seventy first cousins if we did not call them Uncle and Aunty and, dare I say it, call them by their first names! That was a mortal sin. My favourite Uncle Wal, my Mother's youngest brother of fourteen siblings, would go crazy if one of his nephews or nieces did not call him or his brothers 'Uncle'. His fine temper would take over and he would annihilate all in his path. Sound familiar anyone?

I don't hear the terms Aunty and Uncle much reciprocated in non-Aboriginal communities when people are actually related. It's usually on a first name basis to which I recoil upon hearing it. Later I talk to the adult and ask why this is so.

So it is quite clear: if we are blood related then there is no question that you must call me Aunty. This is where kinship relationships creep in, which can be complex to some people but not to us. I remember a colleague at university giving a lecture on kinship and saw, in all his classes, the non-Indigenous students' eyes glaze over, attempting to understand but knowingly not at all. It was just too damn hard for them.

You can be connected to me through family, kinship, country and community. These days everyone sees my community grey hair and straight away call me Aunty. If it is mob then I don't mind at all. I used to occasionally, but passing age 60 has given me much more comfort and leeway. As an Aboriginal woman herein lays the rub. We are dictated by and stooped in our culture. There was never a place for loners in our society and they had to be placed in a kinship and community structure. Relationships were paramount and these influenced how one fitted in.

Likewise with the term 'Elder'. I have never considered myself an Elder but a Senior Aboriginal woman. Some call me Elder too but that doesn't fit well with me. Like many of us we have not had the privilege of our traditional culture and knowledge being passed down, due to the history of colonisation and dispersal of our peoples. I am only an Elder in my beloved Traditional Owner Bidjara and Birri Gubba Juru countries where I have absolute rights to this sacred term. I am also an Elder to my family.

Permission is the key to unlocking the dilemma of Aunty calling. By this I mean *ask first* when in doubt or to show politeness. It is always appreciated. Do not assume because everyone else is doing it, you can. It is not universal. Regularly even Aboriginal and Torres Strait Islander peoples ask me, 'Is it alright to call you Aunty?' My response is usually, 'Yes and thanks for asking.' The only time I do refuse is if they are about my age or older. Unfortunately, I have found this happens with people who have not grown up Black and from opportunistic identifiers. Confusion reigns and they take on their directions from whitefellas. Just because you are Black doesn't give you the right.

Let's talk about age. Don't call me Aunty if you are around my age or weirder still if you are older than me. Yes, I have had non-Indigenous 80-year-olds wanting to call me Aunty, believe it or not. This is so patronising. Obviously my mob know better than that, apart from the ones above whom I have mentioned.

I am now 65 years of age and clearly have earned my Aunty title and status. Over four decades I have spent working in Aboriginal affairs, attempting to build bridges and dismantle injustice to find a place where we can all be at peace with ourselves. I have experienced the peaks and troughs during this time. Sadly, my lifelong efforts still realise this is a distant dream and there is still so much to do.

Whitefellas perceive the stereotype that every woman of mature age is immediately designated the term Aunty. Heck no! Somehow they think they are doing you a favour out of respect but this is quite the opposite. It is disrespect. Don't get me wrong, the whole respect thing is important.

A few of my Aboriginal women friends have shared with me their dislike of being constantly called Aunty in public and private. Great women such as Mary Graham who says Aunty is not a rank. Pat Anderson, N'arwee't Carolyn Briggs, Jo Willmot and numerous others whom I did not have time to get their permission to name them first, but I know they are out there. Ironically most of the women mentioned here have honorary doctorates which indicate their exemplary work in their communities. When I am in a public role I insist on being called Dr Huggins, Dr Jackie or plain Jackie, and never ever Aunty. It's professional and the right thing to do.

The title is compounded these days as last year I was appointed Honorary Professor in History at the Research Centre for Deep History, Australian National University. People don't know how to introduce me now, as Professor, Doctor or Aunty (by those allowed to of course) or all of the above. My preference is to keep the Doctor but I will use Professor on ANU business.

Not every Indigenous woman feels as I do at all. In fact other women love the Aunty title. It gives them purpose, prestige, respect and so on. And that's perfectly fine. We are not homogeneous by any means, nor do we think the same. In fact, my beloved Mother loved everyone calling her Aunty. Sometimes ethical people would ask her permission first, like good friends of mine who were not sure what to call her. She always said yes to their requests.

My further take on this argument is that there is definitely a gender bias. Do I hear our men getting called Uncle as much as our women do Aunty? No. I have sat in meetings and on panels when all the men have been referred to by their first names and all the women as Aunties. This is usually by white public servants, advisors, and other stakeholders. How come?

Some of our male leaders never get called Uncle by our mob, unless they are related, whereas women accept that perhaps this is our role now. Rubbish. Young Black men and women whom I have met for the first time these days call me Aunty regardless. That's okay as I don't have a history with you. I have sets of younger men and women who I knew in their 20s and watched their careers blossom who just call me Jackie, and I adore that. Most respectful. Thank you and I hope you never stop calling me by my first name. You all know who you are kids and I am so proud of you.

I have noticed though that some of you have begun calling me Aunty these days and you need to explain this to me, because I do cringe sometimes over it. We had and still do have a working relationship and you should always called me Jackie. It seems weird to me that you now call me Aunty. Where and when did it change? Your answer is predictable: out of respect or because I have grey hair now, and so on and so on … but really? Tell me.

So if I may reiterate, if you have a professional working relationship with me do call me Dr Jackie/Huggins or first name basis, Jackie. It gets somewhat blurred if you are Indigenous. And by the way the term Indigenous I do use as a personal preference along with Aboriginal and Torres Strait Islander, rather than First Nations. That's a term borrowed from Canada but I do use it occasionally. Now don't get me started on this one as it will take another long essay. Language is important for those who wish to be identified in their own terms.

So if all the above has confused you even more, there is only one thing left to do: *ask first and get permission.*

Waddamooli
Professor/Dr/Dr Jackie/Dr Huggins/Jackie

Notes

Firing On in the Mind

1. K. Gilbert in J. Davis & J. Hodge (eds), *Aboriginal Writing Today* (Canberra: AIAS, 1985), 41.
2. B. Rosser, *Dreamtime Nightmares* (Canberra: AIAS, 1985), 22.
3. Ibid., 23.
4. J. Western, *Social Inequality in Australian Society* (Melbourne: Macmillan, 1983), 205.
5. M. Kennedy, *Born a Half-Caste* (Canberra: AIAS, 1985), 24.
6. R. Broome, *Aboriginal Australians* (Sydney: Allen & Unwin, 1982), 127.
7. B. Rosser, *Dreamtime Nightmares*, 51.
8. Ibid., 20.
9. M. Kennedy, *Born a Half-Caste*, 50.
10. A. Laurie & A. McGrath, 'I Was a Drover Once Myself: Amy Laurie of Kununurra', in I. White, D. Barwick & E. Meehan (eds), *Fighters and Singers* (Sydney: Allen & Unwin, 1985), 83.
11. J.W. Bleakley, *The Aborigines of Australia* (Brisbane: Jacaranda, 1961), 168.
12. R. Evans, K Saunders & K. Cronin, *Exclusion, Exploitation, and Extermination* (Sydney: ANZ Book Co., 1975), 110.
13. A. McGrath, 'Aboriginal Women Workers in the NT, 1911–1939', *Hecate*, vol. 4, no. 2 (July 1978), 8.
14. B. Rosser, *Dreamtime Nightmares*, 53.
15. A. McGrath, 'Before Grog, Before Wages, Before the Japanese War', in B. Gammage & A. Markus (eds), *All That Dirt* (Canberra: ANU Press, 1983).
16. M. Kennedy, *Born a Half-Caste*, 28.
17. R. Broome, *Aboriginal Australians*, 133.

18. M. Kennedy, *Born a Half-Caste*, 24.

19. A. McGrath, 'Aboriginal Women Workers in the NT, 1911–1939', 12.

20. K. Flick, *Sydney Morning Herald* (7 October 1982).

21. E. Windschuttle, *Women, Class and History* (Melbourne: Fontana, 1980), 288.

22. A. McGrath, 'Before Grog …', 78.

23. W. E. Harney, *Life Among the Aborigines* (Adelaide: Rigby, 1957), 14.

24. M. Kennedy, *Born a Half-Caste*, 24.

25. R. Broome, *Aboriginal Australians*, 133.

26. A. P. A. Busia, 'Miscegenation as Metonymy: Sexuality and Power in the Colonial Novel', *Ethnic and Racial Studies*, vol. 9, no. 3 (July 1986), 367.

27. A. Meston, 'First Report on Western Aborigines', 16 June 1897, QSA Col/140.

28. *Daily Mail*, 4 May 1910.

29. E. A. West, 'White Women in Colonial Australia', *Refractory Girl*, 1977, 56.

30. K. S. Prichard, *Coonardoo* (1928) (Sydney: Angus & Robertson, 1956), 51.

31. P. Jacobs, 'Science and Veiled Assumptions: Miscegenation in WA, 1930–1937', *Australian Aboriginal Studies*, 1986, no. 2, 17–18.

32. N. Grieve & P. Grimshaw, *Australian Women* (London: OUP, 1981), 91.

33. A. McGrath, 'Before Grog …', 72.

34. A. Laurie & A. McGrath, 'I Was a Drover Once Myself', 86.

35. B. Rosser, *Dreamtime Nightmares*, 20.

36. G. Nettheim, *Outlawed* (Sydney: ANZ Book Co., 1973), 62.

37. J. W. Bleakley, *The Aborigines of Australia*, 167.

38. Ibid., 168.

39. W. Thaiday, *Under the Act* (Townsville: NQ Black Publishing Co., 1981), 21.

40. M. Hartwig, 'Capitalism and Aborigines' in E. Wheelwright & K. Buckley (eds), *Political Economy of Australian Capitalism*, vol. 3, (ANZ Book Co., 1978), 135.

41. A. McGrath, 'Before Grog …', 69.

42. *Northern Standard*, 5 August 1938.

43. 'The Abo Question', *Northern Standard* (2 August 1938).

44. R. Evans, 'Kings in Brass Crescents', in K. Saunders (ed.), *Indentured Labour in the British Empire, 1834–1920* (Croom Helm, 1984), 204.

45. K. Saunders, *Workers in Bondage* (Brisbane: UQP, 1982), xvii.

46. A. McGrath, 'Aboriginal Women Workers in the NT', 21.

Wedmedi – If Only You Knew

1. B. Sykes, 'Black women in Australia: A history', in J. Mercer (ed.), *The Other*

Half: Women in Australian Society (Ringwood: Penguin, 1975); L. Watson, 'Black is the colour of my soul', and P. Eatock, 'There's a snake in my caravan', in J. Scutt (ed.), *Different Lives: Reflections on the Women's Movement and Visions of Its Future* (Ringwood: Penguin, 1987).

2. M. Burgmann, 'Black sisterhood: The situation of urban Aboriginal women and their relationship to the white women's movement', *Politics*, no. 17 (1982), 23–37.

3. E. Williams, 'Aboriginal first, woman second'; L. Watson, 'Black is the colour of my soul'; P. Eatock, 'There's a snake in my caravan'; in J. Scutt (ed.), *Different Lives: Reflections on the Women's Movement and Visions of Its Future* (Ringwood: Penguin, 1987).

4. J. Huggins, 'Black women and women's liberation', *Hecate*, vol. 13, no. 1 (1987), 77–82; B. Flick, 'Colonisation and decolonisation: An Aboriginal experience', in S. Watson (ed.), *Playing the State: Australian Feminist Interventions* (Sydney: Allen & Unwin, 1990).

5. M. Tonkinson, 'Sisterhood', in *Aboriginal History*, vol. 14, (Sydney: University of Sydney, 1988), 34–5.

Writing My Mother's Life

1. See, for example, the sources available to Bain Atwood (1986) in his writing of the life of Bessie Cameron in the nineteenth century and its consequent inevitable limitations.

2. R. Evans, 'Aborigines', in D. J. Murphy, R. B. Joyce & C. A. Hughes (eds), *Labor in Power* (St Lucia: University of Queensland Press, 1980), 350.

3. G. L. Walsh, *Managing the Archaeological Sites of the Sandstone Belt*, June 1984, QNPWS/AIAS research project, limited edn, copy 10, Central Queensland Aboriginal Corporation for Cultural Activities, Rockhampton.

4. N. B. Tindale, 'Distribution of Australian Tribes: a field survey', *Transactions of the Royal Society of South Australia*, vol. 64 (1940), 302.

5. R. Bundle (Rita's cousin), personal communication with J. Huggins, Woorabinda, 5 March 1986.

6. 'Shaping Lives' Conference, Humanities Research Centre, Australian National University, Canberra.

Reflections of Lilith

1. Letter to the Editor, *Women's Studies International Forum*, vol. 14, no. 5, 506–7.

White Apron, Black Hands

1. This is part of the text in the catalogue of the exhibition entitled *White Apron, Black Hands: A Project on Aboriginal Women Domestics in Service* held in the Brisbane City Hall Gallery, July 1994. The catalogue was produced by L. Black, J. Huggins and L. King-Smith and published by Black Day Dawning, 1994.
2. Cited in M. Tonkinson (1988), 'Sisterhood or Aboriginal Servitude?', *Aboriginal History*, 12, 1.
3. T. Blake, 'Excluded, Exploited, Exhibited: Aborigines in Brisbane 1897–1910', in R. Fisher (ed.) (1987), *Aboriginal, Alien, Ethnic*, Brisbane History Group papers, no. 5, 55.
4. G. Ward (1988), *Wandering Girl* (Broome: Magabala Press, 1988); J. Huggins, '"Firing on in the Mind": Aboriginal Women Domestic Servants in the Inter-War Years', *Hecate*, vol. 13, no. 2 (1987), 5–23; J. Huggins & T. Blake, 'Protection or Persecution? Gender Relations in the Era of Racial Segregation' in K. Saunders & R. Evans (eds), *Gender Relations in Australia: Domination or Negotiation* (Sydney: Harcourt, Brace, Jovanovich, 1992), 42–58; J. Sabbioni, 'I hate working for white people', *Hecate*, vol. 19, no. 2 (1993), 7–29.
5. M. Kennedy (1985), *Born a Half-Caste*, Canberra, AIAS, 4.

Prejudice versus Racism

1. L. Buckmaster, D. Spooner & K. Magarey (2012), *Income management and the Racial Discrimination Act*, Parliamentary Library, <https://www.aph.gov.au/About_Parliament/Parliamentary_Departments/Parliamentary_Library/pubs/BN/2011-2012/IncomeManagementRDA>.
2. United Nations, Human Rights Committee, Consideration of reports submitted by States Parties under Article 40 of the Covenant: Concluding observations of the Human Rights Committee, Australia, 7 May 2009, 3.
3. P. Anderson, AIATSIS Conference, 2017.
4. Reconciliation Australia (2017), *2016 Australian Reconciliation Barometer*, Reconciliation Australia, <https://www.reconciliation.org.au/wp-content/uploads/2017/11/RA_ARB-2016_-Full-report_FINAL-1.pdf>.
5. P. Keating (1992), *Redfern Speech (Year for the World's Indigenous People)* [speech transcript], ANTaR, <https://antar.org.au/sites/default/files/paul_keating_speech_transcript.pdf>.
6. L. Malezer, Co-Chair, National Congress of Australia's First Peoples, Mabo Lecture, 10th Annual Native Title Conference 2009.

7. 'International Day for the Elimination of Racial Discrimination' CESIE, <https://cesie.org/en/news/international-day-for-the-elimination-of-racial-discrimination>.

8. Referendum Council (2017), *Uluru Statement from the Heart*, 26 May 2017, Referendum Council, <https://www.referendumcouncil.org.au/sites/default/files/2017-05/Uluru_Statement_From_The_Heart_0.pdf>.

9. Ibid.

10. Ibid.

11. P. Dodson (2008), *2008 City of Sydney Peace Prize Lecture*, Sydney Peace Foundation, <https://sydneypeacefoundation.org.au/wp-content/uploads/2012/02/2008-SPP_-Patrick-Dodson-.pdf>.

12. Ibid.

13. 'In the two cashless debit card trial areas Ceduna and the East Kimberley regions, 69% and 91% (respectively) of welfare recipients are Aboriginal.' *Social Services Legislation Amendment (Cashless Debit Card) Bill 2017*, National Congress Submission to the Senate Standing Committee on Community Affairs.

14. M. Turnbull (2016), *Closing the Gap statement* [speech transcript], Malcolm Turnbull, <https://www.malcolmturnbull.eom.au/media/speech-to-parliament-on-the-2016-closing-the-gap-report>.

15. G. Yunupingu, 'Rom Watangu', *The Monthly*, July 2016, <https://www.themonthly.com.au/issue/2016/july/1467295200/galarrwuy-yunupingu/rom-watangu>.

Acknowledgements

Many of the articles in this book were published in full or in part in various publications: 'Firing On in the Mind' in *Hecate: The Counter Bicentenary Issue*, vol. 13, no. 2, 1987/88; 'Wedmedi – If Only You Knew' in study materials for 'A Woman's Place in Australia', Deakin University, L. Johnson (co-ordinator), 1992; 'Writing My Mother's Life' in *Women / Australia / Theory*, a special issue of *Hecate*, vol. 17, no. 1, 1991; 'But You Couldn't Possibly ...' in *Breaking Through: Women, Work and Careers* by Jocelynne Scutt, Artemis Publishing, Melbourne, 1992; 'Reflections of Lilith' in *Lilith: A Feminist History Journal*, 1993; 'White Apron, Black Hands' in the catalogue of the exhibition *White Apron, Black Hands: A Project on Aboriginal Women Domestics in Service*, Brisbane City Gallery, July 1994, catalogue produced by Lel Black, Jackie Huggins and Leah King-Smith, published by Black Day Dawning, 1994; 'Respect versus Political Correctness' in *Australian Author*, vol. 26, no. 3, Spring 1994; 'The Great Deception' in *Aboriginal Workers*, a special issue of *Labour History*, no. 69, November 1995; 'Kooramindanjie: Place and the Postcolonial' in *History Workshop Journal*, Issue 39, 1995; 'Oppressed but Liberated' in *Deutschland*, 1996; 'Experience and Identity' in *Limina*, 1996; 'Queensland: Is the Clock Still Back 100 Years?' in *Bringing Australia Together: The Structure and Experience of Racism in Australia*, FAIRA, Brisbane, 1998; 'The Gift of Identity' in *ATSIC News*, February 2001; 'Indigenous Women and Leadership:

A Personal Reflection' in *Indigenous Law Bulletin*, vol. 5, no. 1, 2004; 'This NAIDOC Week, I Want to Acknowledge My Sisters in Jail' in *IndigenousX*, July 2018.